"A wise friend once told me, 'No one should write a book about marriage until they've been married for twenty years.' Then he reached his twentieth anniversary and amended his rule: 'No one should write a book about marriage until they've been married for *thirty* years.' The point is, none of us ever master marriage, because marriage, like the people involved in it, are constantly changing. Yet even though we never master it, there is much we can learn from those who have the wisdom and experience we lack. In *I Still Do*, Dave Harvey has given a brilliant guide to the second half of marriage, to the years that come long after the initial 'I do.' And as someone who is closing in on a quarter century of marriage, I can say it's exactly the book I wanted to read, and perhaps even the book I needed to read."

**Tim Challies**, blogger at Challies.com

"I'm personally so thankful for the wisdom that the Lord has given to my friend Dave Harvey and his willingness to be transparent about the realities of marriage beyond those first few years of blissful adjustments. Going the distance together requires us to face some big moments—defining moments—so that we can learn to love in brokenness and humility. *I Still Do* is a great guide for couples who have discovered that marriage brings complexity but love and wisdom help marriages last. This book is a testimony from three decades of living together before a loving God who fights for marriage. I warmly recommend it!"

**Elyse Fitzpatrick**, author of *Finding the Love of Jesus
from Genesis to Revelation*

"I have written many endorsements, but after reading *I Still Do*, words fail me. This book is so wise, so practically rich, so gospel deep, it's hard to do it justice by a few sentences. But here's what I think is most powerful about what Harvey has written: each page is a mirror. As you look into the pages of this book you'll see yourself, your spouse, the bumps and bruises of your journey, and the inescapable tendencies of your heart. But keep looking and you'll see Jesus—tender, kind, filled with powerful rescuing grace—and you'll remember that he is with you and has been with you in every moment of your journey. Read this book, know yourself, know your spouse, know Jesus, and walk on together with renewed hope."

**Paul Tripp**, bestselling author, pastor, and international
conference speaker; president, Paul Tripp Ministries

"I've long benefited from Dave Harvey's godly wisdom on marriage. And this book came at a welcome time when I needed him again to point me toward hope in Christ. Now I know what book to share with couples married anywhere between five and fifty years as they face new challenges with renewed faith in the God of grace."

Collin Hansen, editorial director for The Gospel Coalition and coauthor of *A God-Sized Vision: Revival Stories That Stretch and Stir*

"I found this book very refreshing to my soul. It's coursing through with the real gospel and the very healthy biblical realism that not all our painful problems are due to our personal sin, but also from living in fallen bodies and fallen societies (like our families) and in a fierce spiritual war zone. Dave Harvey has given us a great gift. Newlyweds will benefit from learning to anticipate defining moments that build a durable marriage. But for those who've been married a while—perhaps a long time—and wonder why it's so hard, why things just don't work right, and may be losing hope, this book is priceless."

Jon Bloom, cofounder and senior teacher, Desiring God

"Here's a book with fresh insights, full of great aha moments, and that actually explores new ground in the complexity of the marriage relationship. Dave Harvey brings a pastor's heart and a theologian's mind to the subject to help all of us learn how we can do a better job of loving each other."

Bob Lepine, cohost of *FamilyLife Today*

"Honest, insightful, earthy, wise, hope-giving. Dave Harvey writes about marriage in a way that is theologically rich without being merely theoretical, transparent without being self-focused, realistic without being discouraging, and gospel-infused without being trite. This book has made my own marriage more durable. Let it do the same for you."

Dane Ortlund, executive vice president and Bible publisher, Crossway

"There are few people who understand the dynamics of marriage like Dave Harvey. After forty-seven years of marriage, I am still learning the lessons that Dave unpacks in this book. If you're wondering if this is an easy read, the answer is no, but not because it isn't well written. It isn't easy because it challenges us in ways that we often prefer to ignore or deny. Dave's insights are biblical, practical, and quite profound. I urge everyone who cares about the health of their marriage (and who doesn't?) to dig deeply into this excellent book."

Sam Storms, pastor of Bridgeway Church, Oklahoma City, OK

"If you want a picture of marriage, don't go to a waterpark. You may see inner tubes floating down a river and become terribly misled. Marriage is more like a marathon; the course is long, the work is grueling, and the couple seems rather out of shape. Of course, many quit. But Dave Harvey wants your marriage to endure and to thrive. *I Still Do* is more than just a training manual; it's medicine for the journey. Whatever you and your spouse are staring at—exciting plans or dashed dreams, a full plate or an empty nest, easy communication or endless conflict—these moments will either derail or define your course. God longs to help you run faster and farther than you ever could alone. Open this book and watch him work."

Matt Smethurst, managing editor of The Gospel Coalition and author of *Before You Open Your Bible: Nine Heart Postures for Approaching God's Word* and *1–2 Thessalonians: A 12-Week Study*

"I want a long-lasting, satisfying marriage that is rugged and durable. Suffering will come. Sin will mess things up. Satan will undermine us. Children will leave. Sex will change. Friendship will wither. Blaming and fights will surface. I want my marriage to not just survive but thrive in a fallen world. Dave Harvey serves us yet again by writing another solid, Christ-honoring marriage book. Get a copy and read it with your spouse!"

Deepak Reju, pastor of biblical counseling and family ministry, Capitol Hill Baptist Church, Washington, DC; author of *She's Got the Wrong Guy* and *The Pastor and Counseling*

"The opportunities for grace pile up throughout the years of a seasoned marriage, as we discover that sinners saying 'I do' is an ongoing commitment in living out the experience of one flesh. For this reason, I am incredibly thankful for *I Still Do*. Page after page, Dave Harvey offers biblical truth and pastoral wisdom for the increasing complexities and uncharted territories of couples growing older together."

Jared C. Wilson, assistant professor of pastoral ministry at Spurgeon College and author of *The Imperfect Disciple*

"I was both surprised and delighted at the humor, honesty, and deep wisdom that Dave Harvey brings to the question of what it means to thrive and flourish within a marriage that has grown out of the early days of heady enthusiasm. This book is packed with insightful, gospel-saturated truths that get to the very heart of our challenges, and gives both hope and practical, down-to-earth strategies to make your own marriage all that God intends. And because it's fundamentally biblical in nature, it's needed for those of us in the UK, and elsewhere in the world, as much as it is for America. I can't wait to get it into the hands of those I serve and love. Simply speaking, this is the best book on Christian marriage that I have ever read."

**Pete Greasley,** senior pastor, Christchurch, Newport, UK

"I praise God for this incredibly helpful book in which Dave Harvey speaks to the heart of marriages shaped by years of defining moments. In reading it I was encouraged and challenged to view my soul, marriage, spouse, and our collective experiences the way God sees them, and to celebrate the difference Jesus makes in all of it. Regardless of where you are in your journey and what you have or have not experienced, *I Still Do* will be of great benefit to you and your marriage."

**Jamin Stinziano,** lead pastor, Summit Church

"Standing at the altar with my husband almost two decades ago, I had no idea what the future would bring. And even though I still imagine myself that young bride, the truth is that the years have changed us. We are different people facing unique challenges in each new season of life. That's why I'm grateful for a book like *I Still Do*. Within its pages, Dave Harvey offers advice and hard-won perspective for marriages like mine that are starting a second lap around the track. But above all, Harvey calls us to run our race relying on the very thing that brought us together in the first place: the grace and kindness of God."

**Hannah Anderson,** author of *Humble Roots*
and *All That's Good*

# I
# STILL
# DO

# I
# STILL
# D

*Growing Closer and Stronger
through Life's Defining Moments*

# DAVE HARVEY

**BakerBooks**
*a division of Baker Publishing Group*
Grand Rapids, Michigan

© 2020 by Dave Harvey

Published by Baker Books
a division of Baker Publishing Group
PO Box 6287, Grand Rapids, MI 49516-6287
www.bakerbooks.com

Printed in the United States of America

Library of Congress Cataloging-in-Publication Data
Names: Harvey, David T. (David Thomas), 1960– author.
Title: I still do : growing closer and stronger through life's defining moments / Dave Harvey.
Description: Grand Rapids : Baker Books, a division of Baker Publishing Group, 2020. |
Identifiers: LCCN 2019028424 | ISBN 9780801094439 (paperback)
Subjects: LCSH: Marriage—Religious aspects—Christianity.
Classification: LCC BV835 .H3685 2020 | DDC 248.8/44—dc23
LC record available at https://lccn.loc.gov/2019028424

20   21   22   23   24   25   26        7   6   5   4   3   2   1

In keeping with biblical principles of creation stewardship, Baker Publishing Group advocates the responsible use of our natural resources. As a member of the Green Press Initiative, our company uses recycled paper when possible. The text paper of this book is composed in part of post-consumer waste.

For my grandchildren,
Ava, Juliette, Weston, Giovanni,
and eventually, by God's grace, the others—
still unborn and known only to God.
This book is written with the prayer that each
of you will be captivated by Jesus
and experience the exhilaration, spark,
and gritty grace of a marriage that lasts a lifetime.

# Contents

## Ending Together

# STARTING T♥GETHER

# Your Journey through Defining Moments

> Marriage is not a thing ordained by men. We know that God is the author of it, and that it is solemnized in his name. The Scripture says that it is a holy covenant, and therefore calls it divine.
>
> John Calvin[1]

Books are great. As a pastor, I have an office filled with them. I've even read some of them. In fact, I've read enough to know there are more good books than spare time to read. This can be maddening.

Since this book explores the uncommon theme of "defining moments" in marriage, you need to know whether these pages connect to your reality right here, right now.

A good book at the right time is a wise companion. It's like a Sherpa for the mind, guiding you up mountains toward maturity— right to the place where God is calling you to go. Good books often

1. Cited in John Witte Jr. and Robert M. Kingdon, *Courtship, Engagement, and Marriage* (Grand Rapids: Eerdmans, 2005), 484.

carry tools we don't even know we need. But they're embedded there in the text, ready for our use when the right moment comes.

A bad book—or one that's read at the wrong moment—can be a waste of time. Its impact never jumps the gap between the author's words and your heart.

With this in mind, let me help you decide whether this book deserves your investment right now.

To do so, I need to tell you a story.

Over ten years ago, I published a book titled *When Sinners Say "I Do."* In that work, I explored marriage as the union of two people who walk down the aisle toting suitcases behind them. New husbands and wives carry the baggage of their lives up to that moment. They carry all the things that shaped them into who they are and all the things that impact what they want out of marriage. But that's not all. Packed in tightly among their hopes, dreams, and family history is their sin.

Imagine going through airport security with enough weapons stashed to start a small revolution. Then imagine the TSA just waving you through, allowing you to skip the inspection completely. Pretty unthinkable, huh? Yet our sin luggage is rarely opened and inspected before our marriage. As a result, the honeymoon and first years can add to the weight we carry. Pretty soon the luggage flies open and our baggage spills out all over each other.

When Kimm and I were first married, I remember being baffled by the ways I behaved and the conflicts we experienced. I remember thinking, "What's happening here? Am I possessed? Or wait . . . is *she* possessed? Oh Lord, is our marriage cursed? I mean, if marriage is so good, why do we seem to make each other feel so bad?"

Over time we discovered that saying "I do" is a defining experience. Getting married opens your luggage. And when that happens, the sin inside can foul the air and soil the relationship. To ignore sin's reality and potency is to deny the very reason Jesus lived, died, and rose on the third day. So I wrote *When Sinners Say "I Do"* (WSSID) to help couples—engaged, newlywed, or in crisis—to understand that when sin becomes bitter, Christ becomes sweet.[2] And marriage gets pretty sweet too.

### After *When Sinners Say "I Do"*

Ten years after *WSSID* was published, Kimm and I celebrated our thirty-fifth wedding anniversary. The milestone prompted me to reflect upon the feedback I've received about that first book. Some readers talked about specific chapters as important moments in their understanding of marriage. But most often the audience was a premarital group, or newlyweds, or folks experiencing some crisis in marriage because they never laid proper foundations.

So I got to thinking, As marriages grow and age, what defining moments do they experience? What are the unique points of trouble and transformation that visit us as our marriages mature—as we navigate the realities of job and financial challenges, keep our heads above water in the kiddie years, raise teenagers or adult children, empty the nest, suffer, age, or prepare for final good-byes?

What moments define a durable marriage?

The more I've reflected on this, the more I've sensed a deep burden to circle back to you with *I Still Do*, a fresh and time-tested perspective on how needs, desires, sin, and gospel applications change as couples move beyond the newlywed years.

For one thing, I've learned that something more than our sin is exposed when we say "I do." Yes, the luggage of our sin required God to become a man and spill his precious blood as the only remedy. But the baggage we bring into our marriage represents more than our sin.

You see, the strength of my first book was also its weakness. I did well to help young couples unpack the undisclosed baggage of their sin. But sinfulness, while central, isn't the only thing that

2. Cf. Thomas Watson, *The Doctrine of Repentance, Useful for These Times*, Vintage Puritan Series (1668; repr., Louisville: GLH Publishing, 2016), eBook, loc. 466 of 1421.

impacts a couple's marital union. As Kimm and I stacked up more and more anniversaries, we began to see these other influences—factors that could not readily be ascribed to our sinful hearts.

Here's one example.

Expressing emotion has never come easy for me. I'm not talking here about the typical "guy thing," though it's true that some men would rather be dragged naked across broken glass than appear to be weak or macho-lite. No, my lack of emotion is much worse. It's something more primal, more visceral. For some reason I struggle to access and define my feelings while I instinctively cap emotional displays. When I came into marriage, I thought denying my emotions was a good thing and conveying them was bad.

> Yes, the luggage of our sin required God to become a man and spill his precious blood as the only remedy. But the baggage we bring into our marriage represents more than our sin.

Ladies, how would you like to be married to a piece of work like that?

Where did my avoidance of emotions come from? Was it a maneuver of my active, sinful heart I'd developed to avoid repenting from selfishness? Maybe. But assuming my avoidance of emotions was the result of sin didn't bottom it out for me. I needed to get in touch with a part of myself that seemed genetically coded in my constitution. I explored and confessed my control issues, but my feelings remained concealed, floating out of reach behind an impenetrable fog.

How could Kimm possibly feel treasured unless light pierced my emotional darkness? And if my visceral reaction to emotional displays wasn't just a result of willful sin, what could it be? My thoughts moved from my heart to my childhood home.

## She Married a Harvey

My dad was a steelworker, just like his father before him. He was also a veteran of the Korean War, and he grew up in a home where he never knew his birth father. If there was a scale of one to ten for measuring emotional responsiveness, Dad would have scored somewhere around "can't find a pulse." I may have seen him cry once—that day when Franco Harris snatched a deflected football to propel the Steelers to victory over the Raiders and clinch a berth in the 1972 AFC championship. I still think the real miracle in the "Immaculate Reception" was the way it broke the dam of emotions pent up in steelworkers all over Pittsburgh.

My mom's tribe came from Scotland, and I think her clan had the disciplined worker genes rather than jovial beer drinker genes. Some of my early memories of Mom include her deck of three-by-five-inch index cards filled with "to do" lists for the kids. I learned to read from those index cards. By eight years of age, I knew how to set a table, dust with Pledge, and apply Liquid Gold to baseboards in a way that didn't stain the carpet.

We weren't feelers. We were doers. It was hardwired into our Harvey DNA.

My parents certainly loved me in their own way, but love wasn't conveyed through an emotional vocabulary. I can't begin to describe my gratitude for growing up in a stable two-parent family where my mom and dad modeled hard work, thrift, determination, and a committed marriage. Like all families, however, we had our dysfunctions.

Ours revolved around this realm of emotions. We lived relatively unaware of our inner world, how the past impacted our present, or how our present circumstances were affecting us. There was no venturing deeply into the feelings of others. Heck, we didn't see a need for it! Love in our home was expressed by doing, not by some flowery concept like "being." And this came to shape my understanding of healthy personhood as a young man. My definition of health did not include identifying or discussing emotions.

I still remember my wedding day, as my brother Wayne and I waited in the church basement for the ceremony to start. As we sat silently, just staring at each other, a stampede of emotions suddenly rushed to my brain like a herd of crazed cattle. This may shock you, but I spontaneously broke down and wept uncontrollably . . . for about fifteen seconds. It was one of the most startling experiences of my life, so out of character that it was creepy.

When I was done, Wayne looked at me and said, "What in the world was that?"

I stared back, utterly bewildered. "Honestly," I stammered, regaining my composure, "I have no idea."

But that wasn't completely honest. Somewhere in my mind I suspected the outburst had something to do with my wedding that day. (*Really, Dave, you think?*)

To this day I live incredibly grateful for the advantages my parents and upbringing conferred on me. But I know now that my emotional disconnect is a weakness in my life and a deficit in my marriage. And as I look at my past, I have to honestly acknowledge that my home was a powerful shaping influence on the way I process emotions. I don't blame my parents or feel like I was robbed. I'm certain they were raised in even more emotionally constricted climates. In fact, I'm pretty sure our home was a Burning Man festival compared to the way they were raised.

> We often encounter weaknesses or personality differences in marriage and instantly try to moralize them.

My point, then, is not to assign culpability for our lack of emotion. Rather, I want to help you identify profound factors that shape *your* marriage—influences that can't so easily be traced back to sinful desires. We often encounter weaknesses or personality differences in marriage and instantly try to moralize them. We assign motives and then ascribe sin to our spouse's actions and omissions. But cultivating a durable marriage involves recognizing that our brokenness is broader than sin. In my case, brokenness included an emotionally stunted home that left a large imprint on the way I experienced and expressed feelings.

## Through Life's Defining Moments

To thrive in marriage over the long haul, we need to care for our spouse as a whole person. That means seeing how God's good news speaks not only to their sin but also to their suffering, weakness, family history, disappointed dreams, physical limitations, and changes in sexual appetite. Lasting marriages need more than just luggage sorting. They need to know how Jesus can help them navigate the complexities of growing older together.

Over the years Kimm and I have had some marriage-defining moments where we just didn't know what to do. Those experiences have often determined our progress and sometimes, quite honestly, have marked points where we plateaued. We learned that falling in love is easy; remaining in love is something entirely different. Kimm and I have often looked back and thought, *Gee, it would have been really nice to know that sooner!*

I'm writing this book to tell you about some of those defining moments—the life-changing experiences, events, and decisions that determine (and sometimes alter) your whole direction. The quote at the outset of this first chapter reminds us that marriage is ordained by God. Yet all the defining moments *throughout* marriage are God things as well; an experience or season in life when God

- presents a decision for truth,
- requires a cost,
- offers a Christ-exalting opportunity,
- grows the soul,
- determines our destination.

I've put a defining moment statement at the head of each of this book's remaining chapters. Some of these statements—such as "Brokenness Is Broader Than Sin," "Sex Changes with Age," or "When Grace Conquers Your Wasted Moments"—may take you by surprise. But each marks a time that is crucial and defining—moments that ultimately give voice to our fear, frustration, and desperation. Each of these moments becomes an invitation from God to transform the core of our being and to deepen our intimacy with our spouse.

Admittedly, most of life is made up of pretty ordinary days where big moments don't exactly break into our monotony. We're not superheroes, spies, or sports stars who have one shining moment to rise above the routines of life. There are no gold medals for what we do. Our days are occupied with carpools, careers, and colon checks. Moments in our world feel pretty ordinary. Growth is about applying truth over time; it's a long, slow obedience.

But the need for ordinary endurance does not eliminate the reality of defining moments.

God presents such moments in the life of every couple. They become doorways to new insights or trailheads that redirect our paths. Some of these invitations will be self-evident; others will be downright astonishing. But one thing remains certain. How we respond to these moments in marriage determines whether we stumble along separately or move forward together toward maturity. As Charles Spurgeon soberly observed, "Failure at a crucial moment may mar the entire outcome of a life."[3]

Perhaps now you're starting to think this book may be important or even essential for you.

I've written it because I don't want you to miss these crucial moments.

### Back to You

If you're holding this book with the hope of going the distance with your spouse, then I want to invite you into a journey. If you read *When Sinners Say "I Do,"* consider this a ten-year checkup.

3. Iain H. Murray, *The Forgotten Spurgeon* (Carlisle, PA: Banner of Truth, 2009), 161.

I'm no expert, and I'm not married to one either. But I'm a husband and a pastor with three-and-a-half decades logged in both roles. More importantly, I think you may discover in these pages that you and I are pretty similar—far more than you may realize. Maybe your marriage has become merely functional, operating like a small business in the service of teenagers, occupations, or retirement goals. Maybe you are in the midst of a marriage crisis, just fighting to hang on to your vows. Or maybe you're maturing gracefully from one season to the next. Whatever your situation, I want to give you a new and time-tested perspective about how God may use these defining moments to make your marriage more resilient, more robust, and altogether more durable.

Really, I just want to write to you about what Kimm and I have learned, and I want you to see how Jesus makes the difference for every decade. He meets us in every defining moment of marriage.

If that sounds like it could help you, then I think this book is worth your time.

# CHAPTER 2

DEFINING MOMENT #1:

# When You Discover Brokenness Is Broader Than Sin

I'm a sucker for simplicity. Give me some simple steps to follow or an easier way to do something, and you're delivering me to my happy place. Our local library now has self-scanning checkout for borrowed books. You waltz up, wave the book, and walk out. I love it. It's child's play. In the history of the world, literacy has never been so simple.

Complexity, on the other hand, I hate. It's a time thief, robbing me of hours I could spend enjoying simplicity. I've got one television, and it has three remotes. Each remote has something like a hundred buttons on it. I'm scared to death to go near those things. Life is complex enough without needing to call tech support to change a channel. Wasting my time should be simpler.

Not long ago, I heard about a principle of logic called Occam's razor. It's the problem-solving principle that when you're presented with competing explanations to a problem, the one with the fewest assumptions is most often true. All things being equal, the simplest option is usually correct. At least, most of the time.

And so it is with marriage. The biggest problem within my marriage—the simplest way to explain it—is my own sin. God has designed the marriage relationship to be part of his change process in our lives. His magnificent goal is to make husbands and wives more like Jesus. But for us to become more like Christ, we must reckon with the fact that we are sinners. In Christ we're wholly forgiven, yes, but we still battle a drive to make our life more about us and less about God.

If we don't lock down this transformational biblical idea, we don't really understand what makes the gospel such good news. If we don't see our sin in all of its stink, we have no context for what Christ accomplished when he died in our place. "The gospel is meaningful for us," says Jerry Bridges, "only to the extent that we realize and acknowledge that we are still sinful."[1] If we don't see our renegade desires, we can forget our daily need for grace and mercy. Although we are new creations in Christ, we still sin every day in thought, word, and deed—and perhaps even more importantly, in motives. Marriage is what happens when *sinners* say "I do."

## Brokenness Broader Than Sin

But saying sin is our biggest problem does not mean sin is our only problem. Marriage is complex, particularly when we add a mortgage, teenagers, in-laws, and, of course, any kind of cat. And this is where our craving for simplicity can sometimes lead us astray.

Some couples nudge their problems toward simplified solutions—categorizing one another's behaviors as either a moral transgression or moral righteousness. Heck, some spouses just slap a "SIN" sticker on the side of every issue

> Saying sin is our biggest problem does not mean sin is our only problem.

1. Jerry Bridges, *The Discipline of Grace* (Colorado Springs: NavPress, 2006), 22.

that irritates. It's a human tendency and certainly not unique to our generation.

Christ's disciples once related a horrific current event to him. Pilate had mingled the blood of certain Galileans with the temple sacrifices. Jesus blocked their impulse to oversimplify the tragedy: "Do you think," Jesus asked, "that these Galileans were worse sinners than all the other Galileans, because they suffered in this way?" (Luke 13:2).

It's the disciples' version of the same diagnosis we use in marriage: "You suffer because you've sinned." We reflexively slice up our own—or our spouse's—behavior into neat categories of good and evil, right and wrong, not realizing that something vital is undermined in our haste to render a verdict.

At risk is our spouse's personhood. We miss seeing them as a whole person—a person full of sin *and* grace, weakness *and* strength; a person with a broken *and* beautiful human body wrapped around an eternal soul. With a thin, oversimplified view of personhood and morality, repentance—and quick repentance at that—is the go-to answer for everything that troubles us. But this doesn't work, because human brokenness is more complicated than corrupted hearts.

> We miss seeing our spouse as a whole person—a person full of sin *and* grace, weakness *and* strength; a person with a broken *and* beautiful human body wrapped around an eternal soul.

In a marriage, hasty oversimplifying can stagnate our condition even as it creates the illusion of progress. It happened to Sully.

Sully has been married to Clara for twenty happy years. His job, though immensely satisfying, required hard work and long hours. Their three teenagers were in the "fits and starts" cadence of walking with Christ, where the backward tumbles often felt longer than the forward strides.

One day, as Sully drove down a highway, his heart began to race. Subtle at first, the sensation grew into a chest-thumping frenzy. A headache followed, triggering flashes of dizziness. Sully, a CrossFit enthusiast, had never, *ever* experienced this before. When the chills started, he began to imagine himself steering the car off the road into the embankment. Not a rational response, he knew, but one that would certainly disrupt this sudden coup within his members. Sully suspected a heart attack and immediately called Clara, who wisely urged him to abandon his plans and head straight to the hospital.

When Sully arrived at the emergency room, his symptoms had largely subsided. After a few tests, the ER doctor sent him home with a referral to his primary care physician. Sully assumed it was just a rogue virus that announced its presence before passing, but within a few days he had two more episodes. The last one delivered an overwhelming sense of doom that sent him to bed for the day. For Sully, the entire experience just made no sense.

That evening, Sully and Clara sat down to talk over what was happening. Once Clara heard more about his symptoms, she explored Sully's lingering anxiety. She listened well, but Clara saw the locus of the problem as the sin of unbelief. In fact, the more they talked, the more convinced she became. If Sully really wanted freedom from the growing oppression of anxiety, he would need to repent. Clara suggested passages for Sully to memorize, lest the anxiety attack him again. They ended their time by praying together.

There is much to commend about Sully and Clara's marriage. Sully was suffering, and he moved immediately toward his wife. Clara, concerned about a heart attack, urged him to go to the emergency room. She also listened attentively to her husband's experiences and directed him to God's Word. They prayed together, believing God was their ultimate hope and deliverer.

Sully and Clara approached the problem like a solid team—moving together, depending on each other, and supporting whatever sacrifices might be necessary to see Sully thrive again.

Is there really a problem here?

Yes, but it's not a problem of affection or intention. It's a problem of scope. For Clara, Sully's mention of anxiety triggered a reflexive diagnosis rather than a process of discovery. She didn't have a category for the kind of panic attacks that were largely unattached to circumstances and required more medical attention. For her, the Bible always simplifies the complex. Panic revealed anxiety, and at the heart of anxiety is *sin*—full stop. Clara knows the Bible is straightforward about how to deal with the sin of anxiety. And since the problem is sin, the solution must be repentance.

Now, Clara is a good wife who loves her husband. She's also the kind of Christian who believes in biblical faithfulness. She believes the Bible works in real life, and she believes God's good news is capable of bringing change from the inside out. And yet Clara had inadvertently adopted a worldview that constricts maturing couples—one where the path from brokenness always leads to personal sin.

It hurts to admit this, but I've done the same thing. We all stick sin labels on our spouse's suffering. When the disciples ask Jesus, "Rabbi, who sinned, this man or his parents, that he was born blind?" (John 9:2), they represent us all.

## Beyond the Heart of Maturing Marriages

It was a lazy afternoon during an all-day meeting. I'll never understand what it is about sitting around a meeting table all morning that makes a man ravenous, but I attacked lunch like I was satisfying a vendetta. Lunch was now exacting revenge, causing my attention to drift sluggishly in and out of the subject matter. Suddenly, a remarkable conversation was kindled. David Powlison, president of the Christian Counseling and Education Foundation (CCEF), was present at the meetings that day, and he was asked to talk about the causes for our behavior—about why we do the things we do.

David was energized by this question. Right away he jumped up, grabbed a marker, and started sketching the diagram below:[2]

"The heart," began Dr. Powlison, "is the most comprehensive biblical term for what determines our life direction, behavior, thoughts, and actions." He described how the heart lies at the center of all human motivation. The heart is the core of our human existence. Proverbs 4:23 (NIV) says, "Above all else, guard your heart, for everything you do flows from it." Jesus said similar things: "Out of the abundance of the heart, [the] mouth speaks" (Luke 6:45); "But the words you speak come from the heart—that's what defiles you" (Matt. 15:18 NLT). The heart manufactures our desires. Our heart's desires reveal our greatest treasure (Matt. 6:21), and they determine what we do (Gal. 5:17–26). Our desires are even what underlie our conflicts (James 4:1).

I'll be honest. At this point, I was still fighting to stay alert. It wasn't just that everything was playing out within the mid-afternoon "dead zone" of an all-day meeting. There was another reason, something a little embarrassing to admit. What David was saying was pretty familiar to me. My biblical counseling training had traversed the cunning and culpability of the human heart—its cravings, longings, desires, and idols. After years of pastoral training and ministry, I felt fairly conversant about this circle. "Check.

2. The images in this chapter are adapted from a diagram in *Psychiatric Disorders: A Biblical Approach to Understanding Complex Problems*, copyright 2015 by David Powlison et al. Used by permission of Christian Counseling and Educational Foundation.www.ccef.org. Dr. Powlison was quick to add that the concept behind the first two circles originated with Dr. Mike Emlet, another faculty member at CCEF.

Got it. Been there, done that, bought the T-shirt." Sadly, my own unwitting commitment to oversimplicity was on parade.

Then Dr. Powlison drew a second circle. "But that's not the whole picture," he went on. "Our heart is *physically embodied*."

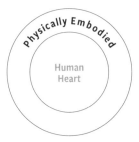

He explained that our heart exists within a decaying frame. We're aging. We have imperfections. We contract diseases. We require sleep every single night. We have senior moments. We're weak, which is to say we have areas of our life where we're not omnipotent or omniscient. We are not God.

I knew just what David was talking about. A few days earlier I'd walked out of Starbucks and tried to unlock my car with its spiffy electronic key. Nothing happened. My mind immediately went dark, instinctively irritated over the wasted day before me. Did I need a new battery for my key (*Do these things even have batteries?*), a new battery for my car (*It has a brand-new battery!*), or was some other unexpected repair necessary (*I hate cars!*)? While I tanked emotionally over the hours I was about to lose calling AAA to get my key repaired, I spied another car in the parking lot that looked eerily like mine (*Wait a minute . . .*).

It's a bad omen when you start your day realizing that your key is fine but your brain is defective. I am weak, and every day there are more clues.

In a broken world, our minds and bodies fail. We are not yet what we will be. There is forgetfulness, joint aches, menopause, depression, cancer. The imperfect chemistry and physiology of fallen bodies can impact our ability to control our desires and respond to our circumstances. And our bodies have a direct effect on our souls.[3] Charles Spurgeon, in a flourish of pastoral preaching, advised his congregation, "Do not think it unspiritual to remember that you have a body, for you certainly have one, and therefore ought not to ignore its existence."[4]

Do you remember Sully? His panic attacks appeared to be entirely unrelated to stress, were triggered at seemingly random times, and were not connected to any known sin. I'm not suggesting his heart was completely pure. There may have been sinful anxieties embedded somewhere in his condition. But seeing our personhood holistically prevents oversimplicity from driving the diagnostics. It was seeing his soul as *physically embodied* that allowed Sully to pursue a physician, start medication, and begin other practical steps that largely eliminated his symptoms.

As Dr. Powlison wrapped up this point, I caught a second wind. Not because the idea of an embodied soul was groundbreaking, but because I sensed Dr. Powlison had some more circles in him. Sure enough, he drew a third.

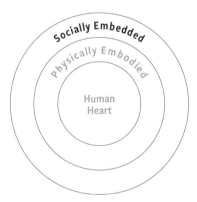

3. D. Martyn Lloyd-Jones illustrates this impact when discussing depression. He says, "Though we are converted and regenerated, our fundamental personality is not changed. The result is that the person who is more given to depression than another person before conversion will still have to fight that after conversion." In *Spiritual Depression: Its Causes and Cures* (Grand Rapids: Eerdmans, 1965), 109.
4. C. H. Spurgeon, *The Metropolitan Tabernacle Pulpit*, sermon #1668, "The Still Small Voice," https://www.spurgeongems.org/vols28-30u/chs1668.pdf.

"There's even more beyond our bodies," David explained. "The heart and body are *socially embedded*." He described how our responses to temptation are always impacted by our situation and story. Growing up in poverty with an abusive father shapes a person in a different way than growing up in a stable two-parent family nestled within a middle-class suburb. As I discussed in chapter 1, growing up with an emotionally distant father can affect the way you process and experience emotions.

Does your spouse come from a family with a history of addictions? Did your husband experience physical abuse? Did your wife experience sexual abuse? Often the older we get, the more we comprehend the impact. In a fallen world, brokenness visits us until we depart.

At this point, I was awake and alert. We were scavenging through the kind of family-of-origin and life-experience terrain that, sadly, my pastoral orientation hadn't frequented. But as a couple grows older, it becomes important for each spouse to better understand the influence of their personal history—to see that past experiences have present influence, that past family life remains a present force on behavior. I thought about counseling situations that I had dealt with or heard about. I thought about people like Callie.

> We must see that past experiences have present influence, that past family life remains a present force on behavior.

Callie had a secret. It had filled her with shame and self-reproach ever since she and her husband, Kent, went on their "humbling honeymoon," the term of endearment Kent used to describe their wedding night. Kent's kindhearted joking only magnified Callie's sense of humiliation, primarily because he didn't know her secret.

Callie hated sex.

It was not a Kent thing. Callie loved her husband and remained deeply attracted to him. She had no regrets about marrying Kent or becoming a mother to their three wonderful kids. They had sex. But Callie still hated it.

Callie had been sexually abused. *If only she had talked to someone about the things her uncle did . . . If only she had given voice to her confusion, her self-loathing, her episodes of crushing depression . . .* But when Callie considered her absentee father, her single mom, and their dysfunctional family, she felt that her unspoken secrets were safer.

Callie had thought marriage might solve the problem. After all, Kent was a godly guy who'd been raised in a Christian home. One year after they met, Kent said, "Marry me," and six months later they were hitched. It all seemed so storybook. Callie figured her body would awaken for her new husband for sure. But it had been thirteen years since Kent and Callie walked the aisle. She still loved Kent, but the abuse had its effects. Callie's body rejected what her mind desired.

When she slowed down long enough to think, Callie felt despondent. "What's done can never be undone," she cried. "I'm damaged goods! My body is hopelessly broken, and I just don't know what to do!"

Helping Callie was not simply a matter of opening up to 1 Corinthians 7 and informing her that Kent, as her husband, has authority over her body. Nor would I start by conveying the urgency of forgiving her uncle. Such an approach would be misguided and foolishly cruel.

Callie needed to know she wasn't damaged; she was the victim of a crime. Actually, many crimes. Callie needed to know that this was not her fault. And she needed to see that God is powerful enough to overwrite her story of sexual abuse with a new chapter—one in which her identity is transformed and her body is reclaimed.

Our past relational experiences exert a powerful sway over our present. They do not *determine* our behavior, but they deeply *influence* how we think and choose. To truly understand your spouse—to know them fully in order to love them devotedly—is to understand their relational past and how it influences their present.

I saw where Callie fit in the "Socially Embedded" circle, and now I was fully engaged. I had no idea where this whole thing was going . . .

## The Circles Keep Coming

"There's still more," said Dr. Powlison. "Our heart, which is physically embodied and socially embedded, is also *spiritually embattled*." He traced the next circle.

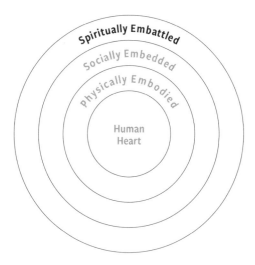

David quoted the apostle Paul: "For we do not wrestle against flesh and blood, but against the rulers, against the authorities, against the cosmic powers over this present darkness, against the spiritual forces of evil in the heavenly places" (Eph. 6:12). He also reminded us about what Peter said: "Be sober-minded; be watchful. Your adversary the devil prowls around like a roaring lion, seeking someone to devour" (1 Pet. 5:8).

The Bible is clear: there are spiritual forces at work in the physical world. No matter how uncomfortable it may feel or how provincial it may sound, it's true. These enemies are hard at work, seeking to influence us away from our heavenly Father and toward the hellish fiend. When you add this spiritual dimension, complications are squared. How does one truly quantify our battle with temptation? How does Satan influence our mind and actions? How are his devices really at work in slander, division, false teaching, wayward cravings, worldly worries? Who controls the accelerator and the brake pedal? Satan influenced Judas toward betraying Christ, yet it happened in a way that didn't diminish human responsibility (Luke 22:3; John 13:2, 10–11).

Adapting C. S. Lewis's classic allegory *The Screwtape Letters*, Ira W. Hutchison describes how the demonic mentor, Screwtape, instructs his young protégé, Wormwood, to deal with a human subject named Mark. Mark struggles with anger, so Screwtape provides Wormwood with the strategy for converting Mark's weakness into blindness.

> Since he is inclined to interpret everything through his needs and wants, you will find much satisfaction in aggravating his judgments of others. His wife and children have their own faults and blind spots. . . . Lead him to magnify the error of their ways. Breed his obsession to take everything personally. Let him feel in his gut that he has the right to have things the way he wants. Blind him to any effort to see things through their eyes.[5]

There are things at work in us that go way beyond nature or nurture. Trivial labels for behavior pasted hastily on our drives and desires don't kick-start change. If we are going to be truly biblical in examining people's acts and omissions, we must not overlook this unpopular category of spiritual attack.

5. Ira W. Hutchison, *Screwtape: Letters on Alcohol* (Kansas City, MO: Sheed & Ward, 1992), 28.

Why? Because our goal is not simplicity; it's biblical clarity. In the next chapter I'll unpack some specific ways the devil seeks to sow deception in our marriage relationships. We do well to remember that when we aim for a lifelong marriage, Satan mobilizes the forces of hell to divide us from one another and rob us of the beauty we've been given.

Dr. Powlison then drew the final circle. I couldn't imagine what it would be.

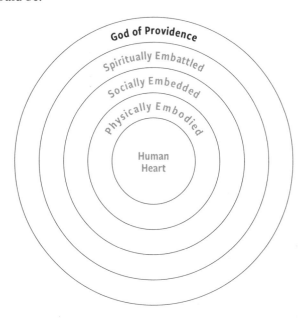

"The most awesome and mysterious circle is the doctrine of *God's providence*," David said. The Bible tells us that God works through all secondary causes to execute his good and perfect will. He encircles our embodied hearts, our social systems, and our spiritual battles with his good intentions and gracious purposes. In every circumstance, he is behind it all, working "for the good of those who love him, who have been called according to his purpose" (Rom. 8:28 NIV). Not one sparrow falls to the ground without his notice, without his care.

Joseph comes to mind. He was an egotistical teenager in a dysfunctional family. His father enabled him. His brothers were so despicably jealous, they sold Joseph into slavery. When you read his story in the latter chapters of Genesis, you discover God's sovereignty over all of the circles. He knew Joseph's heart, his body's afflictions, and the grievous sins of his family. But in the end, Joseph looked back on all of the sin and suffering and could say confidently to his brothers, "You intended to harm me, but God intended it for good" (Gen. 50:20 NIV).

> We do well to remember that when we aim for a lifelong marriage, Satan mobilizes the forces of hell to divide us from one another and rob us of the beauty we've been given.

Job's story sparkles with the same truth. He was embattled by Satan and afflicted in every way. Yet when we read the end of the story, we conclude, "It's all from the Lord—for God's glory and Job's good."

The events of one's life, the activity encompassed within all of the circles, their influence on who we are and what we become—all of these contain defining moments that themselves are lovingly tucked within the care of God's astounding providence. As Philip Graham Ryken writes:

> God is the King of Time. He regulates our minutes and seconds. He rules all our moments and all our days. Nothing happens in life without his superintendence. Everything happens when it happens, because God is sovereign over time as well as eternity.[6]

Dr. Powlison put down the marker and took his seat. I don't even remember seeing him leave the board because my eyes were transfixed on the nested circles. There was beauty in the simplicity, not as an alternative to complexity but rather because of the

6. Philip Graham Ryken, *Ecclesiastes: Why Everything Matters*, Preaching the Word (Wheaton: Crossway, 2010), 80.

manner in which it made complexity beautiful. I'm reminded of an oft-repeated quote from Oliver Wendell Holmes: "I would not give a fig for the simplicity this side of complexity, but I would give my life for the simplicity on the other side of complexity."

The nested circles offered a simplified way to understand the complex influences that shape marriage. They were, in the words of Holmes, "the simplicity on the other side of complexity."

I set down my pen and stared out the window. Instinctively, in that deep corner of the soul that marks memories, I knew this was a defining moment for me. David had given us a brief framework for understanding what theologians call *theological anthropology*—that is, how we, understood as whole people, respond to life in a broken world. This grid would become a tool for my pastoring and parenting, and particularly for my marriage.

### How Does This Defining Moment Help My Marriage Endure?

As I close my eyes, I imagine you finishing that section and saying, "Interesting stuff, Dave. But what do these nested circles have to do with improving or fortifying my marriage?" That's the right question to ask. Let me suggest three answers.

*First, the nested circles help you see the scope of Christ's transforming work.* Essential to marriage longevity is understanding that you married a broken sinner. Your spouse is someone who has been specifically and personally impacted by living in a broken world. At the heart of our brokenness is our sinful separation from God prior to conversion (Eph. 2:1–3) and our ongoing war with sin after conversion (Gal. 5:17).

We all feel this battle. The other day, Kimm said something I arrogantly dismissed. In an exhibition of self-importance, the pride in my heart found a tongue and I spoke. In that moment I was a poor leader, a weak example, and an unloving husband. I was an unthinking Christian, spreading stumbling blocks all over the living room. The Holy Spirit convinced me I had sinned. I thank God that his grace convicted me and sparked a confession later that day. But it was a fresh reminder that I walk through this world carrying a war within me. And as long as I draw breath, this ongoing battle with sin remains my biggest problem.

But my indwelling sin does not define me. The cross made certain of that. Sin resists me, attempting to subvert the activity of God, but my struggles with sin no longer form my identity. I don't think of myself as "Dave the arrogant" any more than I would want you to see yourself solely as "Cindy the abuse survivor" or "Ron the addict." Because of Christ's work, we are now the objects of his love and under new ownership. We're clothed with his righteousness, forgiven for our sins, adopted into his family, and given a new identity. When God thinks about Christians, he remembers the flawless, finished work of his Son, and it elicits his love, joy, and unthwarted blessing.

What does all of that mean for marriage? Christ solved the deepest problem of the center circle, and now his finished work begins to roll back the effects of the fall, beginning with our hearts and spilling over into every other sphere as well. Because Christ is at work redeeming every sphere, we can boldly explore the outer circles without displacing the center one. We do this, for we know that human beings are complex and our spouse is more than a sinner. Knowing my family background doesn't keep Kimm from exploring my emotional life, but knowing the complexities of the way I was raised gives her patience for the journey. And because of what God accomplished in Christ, we can explore the complexity of our problems with hope. We need our Savior for every sphere, and we need him every day.

The circles show us all the ways gospel power is unleashed on the earth. Through his sacrificial death and glorious resurrection, Jesus transforms the circles, beginning with the center and mobilizing outward until "the whole earth [is] filled with his glory" (Ps. 72:19).

Christ's work begins to roll back the effects of the fall, beginning with our hearts and spilling over into every other sphere.

*Second, the nested circles transform our marriage into a place for whole-person ministry.* Through marriage, God invites us to fully know another human being. This only sounds simple. In life, knowing becomes increasingly complex as we move from knowing simple things (like a spatula), to more complex things (say, a tarantula), to things with even greater complexity (our spouse). Ultimately, this principle works itself out to God himself. "The more complex the object," says J. I. Packer, "the more complex is the knowing of it."[7]

Marriage is a quest toward knowing the complex gift God gave you in your spouse. You are to learn who they are as a *whole* person so that you can skillfully love and care for them. This never involves ignoring sin in your spouse, but it does require you to see beyond patterns of temptation and sin to God's larger purpose.

Just like her mother and grandfather before her, Jan struggles with depression. She manages her life through diet and exercise, honest conversations with her husband Dale, Bible meditation, active involvement in her church, and a daily dose of an antidepressant. Jan's condition has become a vital part of Dale's calling. The nested circles have helped him to understand the various factors that contribute to her depression without ignoring or overshadowing her heart. Jan's husband prays for her regularly, ensures she is exercising, encourages her doctor visits, and occasionally challenges her self-pitying temptations when he discerns that Jan is overindulging her depression. The more Dale engages his wife to understand her world, the more he is armed to lovingly offer help in a way that rightly divides her physiological affliction from her culpable heart.

Earlier in their marriage, Dale had some legalistic instincts. He interpreted all behavior in light of Jan's sinful heart, but that never

7. J. I. Packer, *Knowing God*, 20th anniversary ed. (Downers Grove, IL: InterVarsity, 1993), 35.

really helped her. Then Dale had a defining moment. He came to see that our brokenness is broader than our sin. He realized that to fully love Jan, he must deeply know her. Because Dale wanted to love his wife "as Christ loved the church and gave himself up for her" (Eph. 5:25), he spent time exploring each circle to understand Jan more comprehensively. Understanding Jan's story, her family, and her past has also helped Dale to better understand her tendencies and temptations in a way that genuinely edifies her.

Exploring how fallenness affects the whole person has helped Dale to see the fullness of God's love. As the years pass, Dale and Jan feel closer than ever. Yes, they fight and fret. But they are building a more durable marriage because Jan's suffering has delivered an unexpected gift: Jan and Dale both know and are fully known. Their marriage embodies the wisdom conveyed by Timothy Keller:

> When over the years someone has seen you at your worst, and knows you with all your strengths and flaws, yet commits him- or herself to you wholly, it is a consummate experience. To be loved but not known is comforting but superficial. To be known and not loved is our greatest fear. But to be fully known and truly loved is, well, a lot like being loved by God. It is what we need more than anything.[8]

*Finally, the nested circles help us adapt to changes in our marriage.* Next time you see newlyweds, tell them to take a good look at their spouse. Then remind them that if their marriage endures, they will actually live with several different spouses, all of them the same person.

Sound confusing? Most people enter marriage unaware of the seismic changes that will take place in their spouse as the years roll on. Appearance, ideas, preferences, pains—they will morph into something bearing a strong resemblance to your wedding pictures

---

8. Timothy Keller, *The Meaning of Marriage* (New York: Dutton, 2011), 95.

but dramatically different from the one to whom you said "I do." Being married long means adapting much.

Remembering we are embodied souls helps here as well. The nested circles can help us see how our "cleaving" (Gen. 2:24) must adapt to changing needs and aging bodies. It can be hard for honeymooners to understand—largely because it's impossible to pull them apart—but growing old together means that bodies change, desires change, and things just don't work as well . . . or, dare I say, as often!

So we must adapt to each season, knowing that "though our outer self is wasting away, our inner self is being renewed day by day" (2 Cor. 4:16).

In a similar way, the afflictions of one's family of origin can supply important data about our spouse's physical vulnerabilities, mental proclivities, and health trajectory. As a marriage ages, visiting the circles often becomes even more vital, since our fallen condition surfaces with more force and frequency. Paul describes it well as he continues in 2 Corinthians 4:17–18: "For this light momentary affliction is preparing for us an eternal weight of glory beyond all comparison, as we look not to the things that are seen but to the things that are unseen. For the things that are seen are transient, but the things that are unseen are eternal."

## Where We Go from Here

As you come to the end of this second chapter, you may realize you've understood your spouse's behavior in a far too narrow and simplistic way. You may be sensing you need a more holistic and perhaps more biblical vision. You are having your own defining moment.

If that's you, you're heading in the right direction. Let's stick together for a bit longer so I can share some other defining moments. We'll see how blaming our spouse is embedded deep within our DNA. We'll discover how marriage is deliberately designed to reveal our weaknesses so that we might encounter the astonishing grace of God. We'll discuss what to do when our dreams for our marriage leave us with nothing but disappointment. And we'll look ahead to what we might do if we realize we've wasted our life and marriage on the wrong priorities.

If you're curious to hear more, then keep reading. The God who knows you and loves you wants to meet you—in all of your complexity—in those moments. I believe God is at work in you right now as you seek to build a strong, God-glorifying, time-tested marriage. Before we go on to the third chapter, let's look at a chart that helps us to apply and remember the content from this important chapter.

# Defining Moment #1:
## When You Discover Brokenness Is Broader Than Sin

To thrive in marriage over the long haul, we need to care for our spouse as a whole person. That means seeing how God's good news speaks not only to our spouse's sin but also to their brokenness.

|  | The Moment | Our Response |
|---|---|---|
| **The Decision for Truth** | Will I moralize and oversimplify every issue in our marriage? Will I slap a "SIN" sticker on the side of everything that irritates me? | *Or* will I embrace the complexity of brokenness that is bigger than sin—weaknesses such as physiology, affliction, and the changes that come with age? |
| **The Cost Required** | Will I shrink back from caring for my spouse as a whole person because it violates my comfort, pushes me to think deeper, or because I'm afraid that I may appear light on sin? | *Or* will I better understand the influence of my personal history, acknowledging that my upbringing, past experiences, and even the sins of previous generations—while not determinative (Phil. 3:13)—do have present influence upon my behavior (Num. 16:14)? |
| **The God-Exalting Opportunity** | Will I remain willfully unaware of the spiritual battle that is waged against our marriage, simply because it is unpopular or makes me uncomfortable? | *Or* will I grow in prayer and confident trust in God, who works through all secondary causes to execute his good and perfect will? |
| **The Way It Grows the Soul** | Will I miss God's invitation to see that personhood means more than simply the activity of the heart? | *Or* will our marriage be transformed into a place for whole-person ministry where we can love each other skillfully and adapt to changes graciously? |
| **The Way It Sets Our Destination** | Will I settle for a diminished view of Christ's work, thinking he only solves my sin problem? | *Or* will I embrace complexity and see the full scope of Christ's work, allowing his finished work to roll back the fall in every part of our being? |

DEFINING MOMENT #2:

# The Moment of Blame

A few years ago, some museum employees were working with the 3,300-year-old golden mask of King Tut. If that name rings no bells, King Tutankhamun, nicknamed "Tut," was one of the later pharaohs of ancient Egypt's Eighteenth Dynasty, the first dynasty of the New Kingdom period. About a hundred years ago, archaeologist Howard Carter discovered Tutankhamun's tomb, complete with a treasury room stacked to the rafters with golden shrines, jewelry, priceless statues, a chariot, and, of course, the burial mask of King Tut himself. This mask is one of the world's most priceless artifacts. It's one of the best-known pieces from Egyptian antiquity.

But there was an accident . . .

King Tut's beard cracked off of the mask. It remains unclear whether it was bumped, snapped, dropped, or hit with a frisbee during a freewheeling coffee break. But what is crystal clear is what the museum employees did in the aftermath. Rather than reporting the damage and ensuring the mask was properly repaired, the museum team grabbed some Gorilla Glue and pasted the beard back on King Tut's chin. Maybe it was epoxy; I don't know. But the goof didn't end there. One report indicates that the museum employees went on to scrape the leftover glue off with a spatula, further damaging the mask.

This story kills me. It reads like a group of seventh graders trying to avoid detention at any cost, doesn't it? But this debacle was much more serious—and costly. The team of eight museum workers faced trial in Egypt for gross negligence.

Mistakes like this make us crazy. We can go to irrational lengths to hide the ways we've transgressed. You know what I mean. We all have our own stories of "gluing on King Tut's beard" in an attempt to escape responsibility, avoid getting caught, or duck out of being in trouble. Dodging blame is embedded deep in our genetic makeup.

And it's one of the greatest threats to a lasting marriage.

## Our Fundamental Problem

In the last chapter, I argued that brokenness is broader than our sin. I wrote about the danger of slicing up our spouse's—or our own—behavior into neat categories of right and wrong, because doing so can oversimplify our spouse's personhood. I talked about the need to see our spouse as a whole person—a person full of sin *and* grace, weakness *and* strength; a person with a broken *and* beautiful human body wrapped around an eternal soul. This chapter does not back away from that truth, not for a second. But on one thing we must be clear. Just because our brokenness is broader than our sin doesn't mean we can blame our sin on our brokenness.

> Just because our brokenness is broader than our sin doesn't mean we can blame our sin on our brokenness.

Here's what I mean. The nested circles from chapter 2 introduce two competing temptations:

*First, we're tempted to drop the center circle—ignore our sinful hearts—and locate ourselves in marriage as mere passive recipients of all the other influences.* When we succumb to this deception, we blame everything that goes wrong in marriage on aging bodies, family histories, and a diabolical devil.

*The second—and potentially deadlier—temptation is to swap out the center circle for one of the others.* This is a dangerous maneuver, since it doesn't appear to ignore sin's existence. Rather, this deception simply says that sin is not our fundamental problem. Instead, our primary issue is, for instance, our biology, our environment, or our dad's addiction.

We must recognize the complex interplay between our soul, body, relational environment, family history, and our great enemy. But if we want to brace our marriage to stand strong and long, we must recognize *the key* enticement and temptation that vigorously strives against marital success.

Do you know what it is?

The list of sins that cause us to stumble are too numerous to count, but there is one fundamental issue that lies at the heart of each miserable marriage and every devastating divorce since the beginning of time. It's also the trouble behind the debacle of King Tut's beard.

*We have trouble accepting the blame when we are wrong.*

## Moral Responsibility under Attack

Kimm and I live in Florida. Last September we were hit with a hurricane, a little lady named Irma, who unleashed its Category 4 personality on southwest Florida. The results, in many places, were devastating. While Irma is now long gone, the damage it inflicted remains.

In Genesis 3, a hurricane named Satan hit the garden of Eden. The effects of this defining moment remain to this day, and they are more significant than most people know. We tend to reduce Genesis 3 to a story about the origins of sin and brokenness. But that's just more of our tendency to oversimplify. The meaning of Genesis 3:1–13 is broader. The chapter gives us a full tutorial on the character, nature, and tendencies of imperfect people. It doesn't just show us where sin *came from*, it reveals the devious way that sin *operates* within the human heart today.

If Genesis were the *Star Wars* saga, chapter 3 would be like the stolen architectural plans of the Death Star. Except our plans are what have been stolen. And they reveal specific ways we're vulnerable to attack and destruction. These plans show the particular places our enemies—the world, the flesh, and the devil—are most likely to attack.

Sin began with a deception: "Did God *really* say . . . ?" And after the man and woman gave in to it, the deception continued. One of the key ways we're deceived—one of the fundamental ways we remain weakened by the original hurricane—is in our tendency to deflect blame, reject personal responsibility, and ascribe our sinful decisions to others. C. S. Lewis nailed it in observing, "Those who do not think about their own sins make up for it by thinking incessantly about the sins of others."[1]

This dynamic shows up almost immediately after the first wedding. Hurricane Satan hit the garden; the woman sought shelter in disobedience; the man took cover in ambivalence. Both were wrong. Both were dead wrong. But instead of owning it, Adam tossed the woman under the bus and grabbed the Gorilla Glue.

When he blamed the woman, Adam shifted his God-ascribed moral responsibility away from himself and tagged her: "The woman whom you gave to be with me, *she* gave me fruit from the tree" (Gen. 3:12, emphasis mine). This clever evasion reveals sin's nature, a potent desire embedded in every heart. Sin scrambles to shift responsibility, both before God and before others. Our tendency is to hide from moral culpability and make ourselves the victim of others' decisions.

And we don't just blame others. Our ultimate insanity is revealed when we convince ourselves we're also victims of God's

1. C. S. Lewis, *God in the Dock* (Grand Rapids: Eerdmans, 2014), 127.

decisions. After all, it was "the woman whom *you* gave to be with me" who put the fruit in my hand.

When sin knocks, we think everyone except us is guilty. Even God.

In the introduction of J. D. Vance's book *Hillbilly Elegy*, Vance talks about working in a warehouse alongside a guy named Bob. As Vance tells it, Bob was nineteen with a pregnant girlfriend. Despite what might seem a compelling source of motivation, Bob was also a terrible worker. He missed work about once a week, and he was chronically late. On top of that, he often took three or four bathroom breaks a day, each over half an hour.

You can guess what happened. Eventually, the boss fired Bob. In an area where good work was hard to find, Bob tossed aside a good job with excellent health insurance. But that's not what troubled Vance the most:

> When it happened, [Bob] lashed out at his manager: "How could you do this to me? Don't you know I've got a pregnant girlfriend?"

Vance then observed,

> When it was all over, he thought something had been done *to him*. There is a lack of agency here—a feeling that you have little control over your life and a willingness to blame everyone but yourself.[2]

I can relate. When my sin gets going, my finger starts pointing. Now, I thought this problem would disappear or at least diminish in strength after three decades of marriage. But I'm still regularly tempted to jump through the "agency escape hatch"[3] as my defense.

2. J. D. Vance, *Hillbilly Elegy: A Memoir of a Family and Culture in Crisis* (New York: Harper, 2018), 6–7.

3. When I refer to personal "agency" in this chapter, I essentially mean personal responsibility. This is not to deny that sin in a fallen world often finds expression in evil systems and structures, practices and policies. History and present reality are filled with real victims of oppression. My goal in this chapter is not

In other words, I'm still tempted to shift the blame. "It was the woman you gave me, Lord" often echoes in spaces where I've just stood. I'm worse than Jimmy Buffett. Even he doesn't duck behind the woman when lamenting life in Margaritaville: "Some people claim that there's a woman to blame, but I know it's my own d— fault."

We're more like Adam than we think. When sin speaks, it supplies a passive voice. *Wait, me?* "I'm just a bundle of goodness enjoying the garden—walking and talking with God, spreading his glory," Adam says. "The bad things are happening *to* me. It's nobody's fault. Actually, I take that back. It's that woman, Lord. *She* gave it to me!"

In Adam's mind, sin was done *to* him, not *by* him. Personal responsibility was swapped for self-pardon. Under the sway of sin, his self-understanding had only one category—being sinned against. This delusion converts our promises into unfair constraints imposed on us by others. You've seen it; in fact, we all have. The spouse who exits the marriage because "God can't expect me to stay married to a person I no longer love!" God becomes a demanding ogre because Scripture holds us to our vows. We then feel free to discard our obligations, since they no longer correspond to our new narrative. Like King Lear, we abdicate the throne of personal responsibility and instead complain, "I am a man more sinned against than sinning!"[4]

How does this relate to marriage? I think you know. In the defining moments of wedded life, there are often two sinners clawing to gain the moral high ground. It gets pretty ugly: "It's all my spouse's fault . . . and they won't own it!" Our eyes are so intently focused on our spouse that it becomes impossible to see ourselves as anything less than a remarkable specimen of saintly forbearance. I mean, angels are doubtless applauding our character and motives as we patiently labor to help our spouse understand the burden of their offenses, right?

---

to be comprehensive but specific: our tendency as spouses in otherwise healthy marriages is to shift the blame to minimize our sin.

4. Shakespeare, *King Lear*, act 3, scene 2, lines 57–58.

I don't think so.

Have you ever noticed that when we tell tales of our trials and troubles, we're rarely the antagonist? We're rarely situated in the story as a sinner with all of our junk. No, we are these remarkably righteous beings, stumbling passively upon our spouse's struggles with sin. *Me? My role in this relationship is to spread love and mirth wherever I go. My heart is pure. My intent is downright otherworldly in its goodness. Her heart? Corrupted. Her motives? Selfish. Her aim? To stick it to me.*

Pray for me, guys.

Returning to the nested circles from chapter 2, a child repeatedly abused by a family member at home is the victim of a horrific crime of twisted sexuality. Here there is an obvious interplay between being victimized by others, the impact of an unsafe home, and even the evil work of demonic influences. But if that child becomes an adult who abuses *their* spouse, he or she is culpable for those adult choices. As long as we draw breath, our sinful hearts offer the primary explanation for why people love darkness rather than light (see John 3:19).

Hiding in darkness is a chronic problem. And it gets worse as we age. Not only do we have a natural bent toward avoiding blame but, barring a growing affection for God, our willingness to accept responsibility weakens as we grow older. Puritan pastor John Owen observed:

> Not only do we have a natural bent toward avoiding blame but, barring a growing affection for God, our willingness to accept responsibility weakens as we grow older.

People in their younger days naturally have more vigorous, active, and quick affections. As their minds begin to naturally slow down, the edge and keenness is lost. Nevertheless, unless they are steeped in sensuality or lustful corruptions, they will grow in their insights, resolutions, and judgments. If, however, their affections (or inclined and disciplined emotions) are not educated, they will become foolish old people. It is as if the weak tendencies of childhood are never corrected, and lead to greater, more exaggerated forms of weakness in old age.[5]

## Recovering Personal Responsibility

If we want a lasting marriage, we must endure in our attention to this detail. Don't let suffering, cynicism, or sin dilute your moral agency. Don't fall into a way of thinking or living that fundamentally undermines responsibility for your choices. Don't pass the buck to others or to God. As James warns us:

> Let no one say when he is tempted, "I am being tempted by God," for God cannot be tempted with evil, and he himself tempts no one. But each person is tempted when he is lured and enticed by his own desire. Then desire when it has conceived gives birth to sin, and sin when it is fully grown brings forth death. (James 1:13–15)

James tells us that losing personal agency is deadly. And here's one reason: *If we lose agency, we lose the humility God requires* (Mic. 6:8; James 4:10).

Humility is essential to a marriage that endures. A humble acceptance of our own responsibility—an ongoing awareness of our culpability as sinners—makes us more self-suspicious instead of "spouse-suspicious," and it helps us to daily depend on God's amazing grace and sufficiency instead of our own. It reminds us that we are not the Creator but creatures. We are not strong but weak. We have not arrived; we're just pilgrims journeying toward our eternal home.

How about you? Does personal agency have a fixed place in your inner narrative? Another way to ask the question would be this: *Am I growing in humility as a spouse?* Here are five helpful

5. John Owen, *Sin and Temptation*, abr. and ed. James M. Houston (Minneapolis, MN: Bethany House, 1995), 43.

questions to ask for the sake of self-assessment. Think of them as an "at-home" humility test.

1. *How do I respond when my spouse critiques and corrects me?* There is a vital link between how we receive correction and whether we have wisdom. The sage says, "Reprove a wise man, and he will love you" (Prov. 9:8); "A wise man listens to advice" (Prov. 12:15); "Whoever loves discipline loves knowledge, but he who hates reproof is stupid" (Prov. 12:1).

> Don't fall into a way of thinking or living that fundamentally undermines responsibility for your choices.

   This is a really hard truth, because everyone hates criticism, and no one more than me. A friend recently told me of some ways I can improve. I cringed at that for two reasons. First, it brashly suggests I'm imperfect. Can you imagine? And second, it confirms I'm responsible for my imperfections.

   Can you see what's happening? When I bristle at correction, I'm demonstrating a lack of humility. How about you?

   Does your spouse see your desire to grow in wisdom when they provide feedback or critique? Are you known in your family or among your friends for receiving correction humbly, or do folks experience you as stiffening and reacting when such appropriate criticism comes your way?

2. *How do I respond when my spouse sins against me?* This is the shoe being on the other foot. If you're married, it's inevitable. At some point you'll be at the blunt end of your spouse's sin. Here's one thing I've learned in marriage: how I relate to being sinned against—or when I think I'm sinned against—reveals my true grasp of the gospel.

   Do you tend to retaliate or give yourself special permission to be angry and cynical toward your spouse when they sin against you? We can all relate to these temptations, but I'm talking about your actions. Examine yourself and remember how Christ responded to us when we acted as his enemies (Rom. 5:10). He demonstrated humble, persevering love. Don't ever forget: "while we were still sinners, Christ died for us" (Rom. 5:8).

3. *How do I describe my largest internal obstacles? Do I tend to use words that acknowledge my personal responsibility when I sin, or do I deflect and shift the blame?* This is our penchant for creating a soft, amoral world. We tend to present an existence where, when I describe myself, I don't really need a Savior—just self-improvement or self-understanding. But this hijacks our ability to share in the gospel's benefits. As Jerry Bridges says, "To benefit from the gospel every day, then, we must acknowledge that we are still sinners."[6]

Are you like me? If I become angry over something, I prefer to avoid biblical words like *anger* and *bitterness* because they're loaded with moral freight that stings. I'd rather mention in passing that I was feeling *moody, touchy, irritated, frustrated,* or *oversensitive.* In fact, maybe I think I woke up *stressed out, ticked off, tense, edgy, annoyed,* or *testy.* You get the point. Those words work well as descriptors, but they have little moral bite.

The Son of God didn't shed his blood because I'm grumpy or high-strung. He died because I'm a selfish and angry rebel.

4. *Do I flee to Christ when I become aware of sin?* "For as in Adam all die, so also in Christ shall all be made alive" (1 Cor. 15:22). Christ came as the last Adam (1 Cor. 15:45–48), obeying God's law in all things and at all times—whereas the first Adam was unable to comply with

6. Jerry Bridges, *The Discipline of Grace: God's Role and Our Role in the Pursuit of Holiness* (Colorado Springs: NavPress, 2006), 22.

one simple restriction. The record of Christ's perfect obedience then became the bankroll of righteousness that was reckoned to us (Rom. 4:23–25). This means that when we sin, we don't need to proudly protect the illusion of our perfection or atone for our sin by doing good works. The last Adam whispered "It is finished" at the moment of his death so we could live an abundant life and enjoy an abundant marriage until we go home to be with him. Humble people flee to the Savior in this life so they can celebrate his glory in the next (1 Pet. 4:13).

5. *Am I growing more amazed by grace?* Paul wrote to the Roman church, "So I am eager to preach the gospel to you also" (Rom. 1:15). The implication is profound. The good news isn't just for unbelievers but for those who are already a part of a thriving church. The gospel is not just the way we begin the Christian life; it's how we grow as Christians. It's easy for us to lose track of this simple truth. Responding in faith to the gospel gives us a new heart with new desires to honor God, repent of sin, love our spouse, and humble ourselves before them.

So ask yourself: *Am I able to see my daily need for Christ's love and gospel renewal? Am I amazed at Christ's sufficiency to meet me exactly where I'm hurting and struggling? Am I growing in awareness of how the gospel applies to my specific sins? Am I moving toward my spouse to confess these sins? Am I expressing gratitude to God for his astounding pardon and power?*

## Scoring Your Soul

How did you do?

Here's the thing. As couples, we have to decide which Adam we will follow. In a defining moment of his life, the first Adam could only see himself as sinned against. But being sinned against is not typically the biggest problem we encounter each week. Since the catastrophic fall in Eden, the biggest problem has been the way we shift responsibility. The first Adam lost his agency; the last Adam, though innocent, took the blame for all who call on his name. If that thought humbles you, your test score may be improving.

The road of humility is open to every husband and wife who are willing to see and admit their desperate need for grace. Standing responsible before God is the painful precondition to standing forgiven by God. This is a truth I knew when I first started out, but I wish I'd known it more deeply and on the level of experience. Over the years, I've learned that accepting blame actually strengthens my marriage. Because Christ took the blame for me and my status is secure in him, I can accept the blame for my sin and experience the joy of forgiveness.

> The road of humility is open to every husband and wife who are willing to see and admit their desperate need for grace.

Experiencing that forgiveness from God and then extending it to your spouse will fortify your marriage with grace to go the distance. We'll see this pattern throughout this book. Over and over, God holds out his promises to those who accept their agency and acknowledge their need for the Savior. He strengthens those who embrace their weakness and own their sin. Will you accept responsibility and then take your faults to Christ again and again? Will you walk that road to him?

I want to walk that road. If you do, too, check out the chart on the next page to further explore the most devastating sins behind crumbling marriages. Then, in the next chapter we'll take a closer look at another defining moment in which God's grace makes every year of marriage even sweeter.

# Defining Moment #2:
# The Moment of Blame

The list of sins that cause us to stumble are too numerous to count, but there is one fundamental issue that lies at the heart of each miserable marriage and every devastating divorce since the beginning of time.

| | The Moment | Our Response |
|---|---|---|
| **The Decision for Truth** | Will my starting point for the problems in our marriage be to blame my spouse? | *Or* will I humbly accept the blame when I know I am wrong? |
| **The Cost Required** | Will I prosecute my spouse for where they may have contributed to the problem? | *Or* will I humbly look for my own contribution and accept my responsibility for sin? |
| **The God-Exalting Opportunity** | Will I submit to the lie that I'm a victim of God's decisions? | *Or* am I able to see that sin set the stage for the Savior's life, death, and resurrection? Am I amazed at Christ's sufficiency to meet me exactly where I'm struggling? |
| **The Way It Grows the Soul** | Do I bristle at correction? Do I tend to retaliate or give myself special permission to be angry and cynical toward my spouse when they sin against me? | *Or* do I consider what's being said, humbly receive reproof, and remember how Christ responded to me when I acted as his enemy (Rom. 5:10)? |
| **The Way It Sets Our Destination** | When I sin, do I proudly protect the illusion of my perfection or try to atone for my sin by doing good works? | *Or* do I flee to the Savior in this life so that I can celebrate his glory in the next one (1 Pet. 4:13)? |

DEFINING MOMENT #3:

# The Moment of Weakness

A shaft of light from the setting sun found the crystal wine glass in Erin's hand. A rainbow diffused across the table. To recline at this exquisite, five-star restaurant for their tenth anniversary was a dream come true. To have a bayside table at sunset seemed like, well, heaven itself had phoned ahead to make the reservation. Kenny raised his glass for a toast. "May the remaining decades be easier than the first!"

Erin lifted her glass to complete the custom, a warm smile spreading across her face. "Marriage is simply the hardest thing I've ever done," she said wryly, "but I would marry you again in a heartbeat. To *us*!"

The dinner was delicious. They conversed about how they first met, the wedding, and their early mistakes in marriage. "I wondered what marriage would look like after the first ten years," Erin said wistfully.

"Excuse me," came a voice from behind her. It was the host who had escorted them to their table earlier. "You are Kenny and Erin, celebrating your tenth anniversary, no?" Kenny and Erin both nodded. "These two gifts were left at the door for you by an unidentified man."

Kenny and Erin looked warily at the host, then at each other. Finally they eyed the two small boxes, identical in size and wrapping, that sat awkwardly at the table's edge, a single card between them. By the time Kenny and Erin looked up to ask more about the bringer of these mysterious gifts, the host was gone.

"I'll bet it's the office," said Kenny. "They knew we were celebrating our anniversary and they probably figured out where we were having dinner. It's a way to praise the best talent. Classy move."

"My dad knew too," said Erin hopefully. "It could be from him."

Kenny grabbed the card and handed it to Erin. "You do the honors!" Erin opened the envelope and read the card aloud:

*"For Erin and Kenny—to make you strong and your marriage last long! Love, Jesus."*

Kenny and Erin just stared at each other. Was this a joke? Their suspicion quickly gave way to curiosity. *Why would someone bring them a gift signed from Jesus? What could it be? How could two boxes help their marriage grow long and strong?* They each grabbed a box and tore it open.

What they found inside was a pair of thorns, grimly sharp to the eye, each strangely customized for the one who opened the box. Kenny and Erin quickly placed them back on the table. Together they stared unblinkingly at the two thorns nestling undisturbed in their boxes like a sleeping viper—silent, venomous, dangerous.

Kenny swept up the note and reread it. "To make you strong and your marriage last long." He looked at Erin and said, "What in the world does a thorn have to do with a lasting marriage?"

## The Weakness Defense

Paul wrote the epistle we call 2 Corinthians during a time of great personal turmoil. A group he calls the "super-apostles" (11:5; 12:11) was planning a coup in the Corinthian church. Their strategy was a frontal assault. The goal was to subvert Paul and seduce the church over to their leadership. It was a hostile takeover dressed up in spiritual jargon.

Have you ever been in a position where forces outside of your control are undermining you or someone you love? Live long enough and everyone encounters super-apostles. They come in many shapes and sizes. In a marriage, it may be seductive voices tempting a spouse away from the family. For leaders, it may be unexpected opposition that undermines our credibility. For parents, it may be the wrong friends at the wrong time for our kids.

Paul couldn't shake these guys. They were pre-internet trolls, who assaulted Paul's competence and credibility. Their attack was hardly subtle. In their view, Paul's leadership presence was unremarkable (10:10) and his preaching substandard (11:4–6). They said his best leadership was seen only in his letters; they said Paul was most courageous when he was away (10:2). They also tagged Paul with teaching for free, a scandal in ancient times, since the best measure of true teaching talent was steep fees (11:7). If all that didn't prove their point, these false leaders claimed Paul had no supernatural experiences, which many people believed were necessary to validate his true spiritual authority.

The primary charge leveled against Paul could be summarized in three simple words: *Paul is weak!*

So Paul finds himself between the rock of his critics and the hard place of his people, an awkward position for any leader. Paul must defend himself and give an account for his ministry. Second Corinthians 10–13 records Paul's defense, and here's where things get interesting:

> So to keep me from becoming conceited because of the surpassing greatness of the revelations, a thorn was given me in the flesh, a messenger of Satan to harass me, to keep me from becoming conceited. Three times I pleaded with the Lord about this, that it should leave me. But he said to me, "My grace is sufficient for you,

for my power is made perfect in weakness." Therefore I will boast all the more gladly of my weaknesses, so that the power of Christ may rest upon me. For the sake of Christ, then, I am content with weaknesses, insults, hardships, persecutions, and calamities. For when I am weak, then I am strong. (12:7–10)

Paul rolls out a paradox—an apparent contradiction—that seems utterly nonsensical at first blush. Paul makes weakness his defense. His argument unfolds this way: "You think I'm weak? Well, I've got wonderful news for you. I'm weaker than you could ever imagine. I'm gloriously weak! In fact, I want to *boast* about my weakness."

Say what?!

## Defining Weakness

Like Paul, we are weak. In fact, *marriage is the union of two people on a journey to discover their weakness.* The goal of such an admission is not self-loathing. That would be like saying the key to spiritual maturity or marital health is reciting the narrative of our failings to any who will hear it. It's something different from self-criticism. To understand why Paul would use this mysterious defense, we must grasp the sensational center of our weakness.

At its core, weakness is *an experience of inability that requires dependence on God.* We experience inability, or weakness, in at least two ways: deadly inability and daily inability.

### Deadly Inability

Weakness is a reality in life and marriage because we are not God. We are creatures, not the Creator. We are finite and live with limitations. But it's not merely that we're limited as creatures, and that we're not as smart or powerful as God. No, we are also fallen. We have sinned. Before Christ, we needed forgiveness; we needed to be born again. Apart from Jesus, we deserve wrath. Our problem is fatal. We are spiritually dead—that is, morally unable to do anything to help ourselves. We are weak, and we desperately need the help of One who is consummately strong. When we were dead, we needed Jesus, the Savior, to do for us what we were incapable of accomplishing in our own strength. Scripture confirms this when Paul writes, "Even when we were dead in our transgressions, [God] made us alive together with Christ" (Eph. 2:5).

> Weakness is a reality in life and marriage because we are not God.

When Paul says, "We preach Christ crucified, a stumbling block to Jews and folly to Gentiles" (1 Cor. 1:23), he's reminding us that the cross is a stumbling block and folly precisely because it rendered human ability totally irrelevant in the work of salvation. It made *deadly inability* the connecting point for grace. Do you remember coming to Christ? We weren't trophies of creation presented to God because we had a spit-shined life and earned his approval. No, we were unpolished, dinged, and dented relics, marred by a life of sin and tossed in the basement. When it comes to inner goodness or outer good deeds, we were hopelessly disqualified from self-salvation.

Trophies don't need a Savior. Weak sinners need a Savior.

It's why the richest and most celebrated people in the world rarely find their way to Jesus. Wealthy and influential people find it hard to embrace their deadly inability. Commentator David Garland describes it this way:

> God chose the foolish because the wise thought the cross was sheer folly as a means for saving the world, the weak because the strong thought they were powerful enough without God, and the low and despised because the high and mighty did not care to debase themselves by attaching themselves to a crucified God. The foolish, weak, and despised, however, respond more readily to the shame of the cross because they themselves are already shamed. Unlike the powerful, those who are deemed foolish and weak are amenable to receiving the paradox of divine weakness that conveys strength.

They respond more readily to the shame of the cross because they themselves belong to the shamed.[1]

### Daily Inability

But weakness is not merely confined to salvation, as if we're desperate for God before Jesus but then convert into superhero specimens of strength. Weakness is also *daily inability*—the areas of limitation, vulnerability, or susceptibility that require reliance on God. Weakness represents those places in life where we're reminded we're not kingdom-ruling conquerors exercising omniscience, omnipotence, and omnicompetence at will. Not even close!

We are the fallen and frail who forget meeting times, wreck our cars, and mistakenly leave the doors open to invite all manner of beasts and insects to become residents in our home. You know what I'm talking about. We are the oversleepers, the overeaters, the bill-forgetters, the "Oh-Lord-what's-that-smell" people. We are weak!

Our frailty is also quite customized. Think about your marriage. For us, Kimm has a bad knee; I travel with a back pillow, compliments of lower back arthritis. Think out beyond your family to the world. People have affliction—physical, emotional, or mental—uniquely stamped on them. The first US president, George Washington, had some serious dental issues and lost all of his teeth; Winston Churchill had a heart condition that uncorked a coronary during a White House visit; Mother Teresa had lung and kidney problems; Abraham Lincoln fought depression. Each of us has distinctive incapacities and health proclivities that seem factory-installed within our frame.

> We are the oversleepers, the overeaters, the bill-forgetters, the "Oh-Lord-what's-that-smell" people. We are weak!

1. David E. Garland, *1 Corinthians*, Baker Exegetical Commentary on the New Testament (Grand Rapids: Baker Academic, 2003), 76.

Yet mysteriously and remarkably, our weakness—our daily inability—becomes a channel for the movement of God. Rather than condemning us for our inability, God chose to make our weakness the place where his strength would prevail. As John Stott once observed, "God's power operates best in human weakness."[2]

## God's Purpose in the Thorns

Remember Kenny and Erin's strange anniversary gifts? The apostle Paul received a similar gift. It's how he learned the paradoxical lesson that God channels his power through our weakness. Paul's defense takes an extraordinary turn in 2 Corinthians 12. To these self-assured, brand-promoting, world-loving super-apostles, Paul begins to relate a supernatural experience. "I know a man," Paul begins (12:2). Immediately, we see this story will look different from the tales of Paul's critics. Paul is reluctant to gain recognition or credibility from his spiritual experiences, so he introduces himself anonymously. His reasoning is pretty straightforward: "I refrain from [boasting], so that no one may think more of me than he sees in me or hears from me" (12:6).

If you're ever looking for a quick self-test on how "Pauline" you appear, just ask yourself, "Am I concerned that people are thinking too little of me or too much of me?" Paul was always concerned with the latter. How about you?

Paul goes on: "And I know that this man was caught up into paradise—whether in the body or out of the body I do not know, God knows—and he heard things that cannot be told, which man may not utter" (12:3–4). Paul was caught up into the third heaven, where he heard inexpressible things. And to keep him from being too elated or excessively proud, Paul was given a thorn.

There's plenty of speculation about the exact nature of this thorn. Some commentators suggest it was an illness, others say

2. John Stott, *Basic Christian Leadership: Biblical Models of Church, Gospel and Ministry* (Downers Grove, IL: InterVarsity, 2002), 38.

persecution, and still others say a physical malady like an eye condition or a speech defect. We really don't know. But we know enough. We know, for instance, that this thorn became a substantial affliction. Why else would a guy who suffered the horror of thirty-nine lashes on five separate occasions, who was beaten with rods three times, and who once suffered stoning (2 Cor. 11:24–25) need to persistently appeal to God for deliverance from it? Paul tells us he pleaded with the Lord three times that it would leave him (12:7).

Whatever this thorn was, it pierced Paul deeply. The thorn had Paul's number.

But look closer at verse 7. When Paul says that "a thorn was given me in the flesh" (2 Cor. 12:7), most commentators agree that the thorn-giver was God. This is why the thorns for Kenny and Erin in my parable above came tailored from Jesus. On one hand, this makes sense, doesn't it? Why would sin or Satan want to keep Paul from being too conceited? They wouldn't. No, God himself pressed this thorn into Paul's flesh. God used a customized affliction—one that would not go away—to restrain Paul and keep him grounded. It made him weak, desperately weak. And this weakness drove him back to God.

But verse 7 says more. The thorn was also "a messenger of Satan to harass" Paul. Somehow the thorn was both the work of the devil and ordained by God. In other words, God used Satan to protect Paul from pride. Think about that. It's mind-blowing. Jesus used the devil to produce godliness in Paul.

Reflect on that the next time you open a thorn on your anniversary. Think about it the next time it feels like your marriage is under assault by the enemy. It may be that God has fitted this weakness for your marriage to make you more desperate for him. It may be that your spouse is ill or you have a child who's been diagnosed with a disability. It may be that your family has a kid or two more than your budget can handle. It may be a financial thorn—a portion of your income is going right back out to pay for student loans, child support, back taxes, or medical bills. It may be that past sexual experiences are creating present sexual complications in your marriage.

Whatever it is, don't sanitize it. Paul wasn't afraid to recognize his thorn as a messenger from the evil one. But, like the crown of thorns pressed on Christ's head, Paul saw that God had a good and glorious purpose behind the pain.

In the parable I told at the beginning of the chapter, Kenny asked an understandable question: "What in the world does a thorn have to do with a lasting marriage?"

Paul helps us begin to see the answer. Thorns produce weakness. And thorn-constructed weakness creates the fruit necessary for marriages to go the distance; fruit achieved in no other manner than by flesh-splitting pain.

## Thorns Carry a Promise

God doesn't send thorns to inflict pain at random. Weakness in itself is not a virtue to God. And while God does use thorns to help us depend on him more, that's not their only purpose. God also uses thorns to connect us to his strength. Weakness is the place where we meet God in our inability and discover his remarkable power.

> God also uses thorns to connect us to his strength. Weakness is the place where we meet God in our inability and discover his remarkable power.

"God gave me three wonderful babies, and they are precious beyond words." Ellen spoke these words with eyes that were brimming with tears. "But the baby weight! Twenty-five cursed pounds that seem to defy every exercise and diet I throw at them. It makes me feel unattractive and undisciplined . . . and our sex life is on a ventilator, gasping for air!"

Ellen never imagined the collateral damage involved with being pregnant three times. Everything stretched, but the elasticity was gone. She hated every ounce of the weight she'd gained. Getting naked and becoming self-forgetful enough to enjoy sex seemed like another life. Her body felt like an old car—high mileage, too many repairs, and substantially larger than the newer models.

In marriage, thorns don't pierce only one party. Our spouse may get pricked, but both of us bleed. Ellen's husband tried to tell her the weight didn't matter. He insisted she was still beautiful, still sexy, still desirable. But this just frustrated her more. Ellen prayed many times, but nothing changed. God seemed to be saying no. The thorn of her weight pressed deep.

Remember, our thorns aren't mass-produced for sale at Walmart. They are highly personalized, encoded with a customized purpose for each of us. And we often experience the presence of the thorn but don't know its purpose.

God may have allowed Ellen's weight gain to suppress vanity or an idolatry of her appearance. Perhaps God was at work cultivating an inner beauty as the thorn made her bleed. Maybe this was about her marriage. Perhaps there were lessons of love God wanted to nurture in Ellen and her husband, teaching them that over time sex should be less about physical attraction and more about being together. Perhaps God was at work to grow her husband into a man who knows how to encourage his wife even when she hates her body.

Paul's thorn came with no clearly discerned purpose but rather with a promise: "My grace is sufficient for you, for my power is made perfect in weakness" (2 Cor. 12:9). Grace comes to those who redirect their attention from what God denies (an immediately discernible purpose) to what God supplies (a firm promise).

> Grace comes to those who redirect their attention from what God denies to what God supplies.

Eventually, Ellen's gaze shifted, and her husband's did too. They realized they were living thorn-centered rather than grace-centered lives, and they began to take small steps together. As the weeks passed, Ellen received "sufficient grace" to change the way she viewed herself. The power to change her perspective wasn't overwhelming, just sufficient. In time, her self-consciousness about her body gave way to a growing awareness of where God seemed to be working. She began to see sex as God's gift in every season, whether bodies are growing larger or smaller. And she learned to be thankful. Though she may not have liked her proportions, she had achieved those dimensions, in part, because of the miracle of three children.

On those dark mornings after stepping off the scale, Ellen couldn't see that her thorn carried a transformational promise. She now lives more confident and hopeful for change in her marriage because God's power is working through her weakness. In fact, the thorn of Ellen's weight is helping her to see the world differently.

## Thorns Change Our Boast

I have a confession. In our first few years of marriage, I saw myself as God's gift to the institution. I looked around and thought, *You know, as a brand, marriage is taking a pretty serious hit. What's needed is some fresh blood, some innovative zeal from a new generation of Christians . . . guys just like me!* I imagined the ways God might use our marriage—exalting the wisdom of biblical gender roles, establishing a potent specimen of marital godliness, or spotlighting my leadership savvy. It would be my starring role!

But getting married didn't make me sparkle. It exposed my weakness. In regretful ways, I trusted in my own strength and what that strength could produce. To keep me from being too elated by my strengths, God gave me a thorn that confounded my leadership and brought my self-assessment back to earth. The thorn was a job for which I was equal parts underqualified and overconfident. As you would expect, it became a perfect storm for revealing some shabby foundations in my life.

My goals going in included getting a quick promotion, the praise of peers, groundbreaking advances, impressive salary hikes, and senior executive status. And that would be just in my first year! Looking back, I realize my impact level on the organization was pretty unremarkable. My quick promotion? A dozen bosses above me could have been hit by a bus and I still would not have made the short list. Moreover, my ignorance was epic. The learning curve toward real progress spanned the height of Everest. But that didn't keep me from dreaming.

What I lacked in experience and self-awareness, I made up for in hard work and long hours. Then it happened.

*"You missed our anniversary."*

I sat staring at Kimm, trying to make sense of what she'd just said. "Remember, our third anniversary? It was yesterday," she said flatly. "You missed it. But don't worry, it was pretty boring for me too."

My eyes filled with tears. I had been working so hard that I completely missed the arrival and departure of that momentous day. Never, *never* in a million years did I see myself as an anniversary-skipping kind of husband. Not when I tried so hard to cover all of my bases. Not when I was throwing my best leadership at life.

But it happened. In my ambition to excel, I failed to prioritize our marriage. I failed to honor my wife. "I'm so ashamed," I whispered through tears. "Please forgive me."

"Of course I forgive you," Kimm responded. "You've been working like a lunatic. Let's celebrate it tonight!"

My thorn was an opportunity that far exceeded my capacity. Then God hand-delivered a thorn that exposed my three selves: *self*-reliance, *self*-confidence, and *self*-sufficiency. Under the elated glare of this corrupted trinity, I had lost sight of a far higher priority than my job. Staring at a missed anniversary through the lens of my wife's gracious forgiveness flipped a switch in my mind. I can't do it all, cover it all, or remember it all. I'm not God; I'm a broken vessel who needs the Potter's touch every day. The illusion of Dave as a consistently strong and attentive husband had to be downgraded. I'm not omnicompetent. I'm really a weak man who needs a strong Savior, so "I will boast all the more gladly of my weaknesses, so that the power of Christ may rest upon me" (2 Cor. 12:9).

## The Unlikely Grace of Unexpected Power

Kenny and Erin's customized thorns came through an unexpected employment change and the impact it had on their finances. Kenny had grown up in a single-parent family with a mom who worked two jobs to ensure her kids had food and clothes. When Kenny proposed to Erin, he told her he would dedicate his life to ensuring their family never knew want. Their first ten years seemed pretty easy. Kenny's business grew and Erin worked part-time whenever she desired. God was faithful and the lack Kenny feared never arrived.

No one saw the crash coming. An emerging technology began to consume Kenny's market share. Within four months, revenue was down 33 percent, and it threatened his company's very existence. In an audacious countermove, Kenny borrowed against his house and updated his technology to stay ahead of the curve. But it was too late. He couldn't keep up. Bankruptcy was the only option.

Kenny never dreamed life could deliver this kind of nightmare. It was like someone lit a dynamite stick and tossed it into the middle of Kenny and Erin's world. Everything in their universe had been strong—their financial position, their community standing, their credit score, their business connections. Now it was ruined. Kenny and Erin were suddenly shutting down credit cards, canceling vacations, and pulling their kids out of private school. Even after desperate measures, Kenny still wasn't sure they could keep their house.

Had Kenny and Erin now opened the boxes from their tenth anniversary, they would have discovered the anniversary thorns were missing. The Giver had removed the gifts from the containers and implanted them deep into Kenny and Erin's flesh. They didn't realize it yet, but their newfound weakness was truly a gift from Jesus. The razor-sharp points would carry divine purpose, working mysteriously to make Kenny and Erin humble, God-minded, and desperate for Jesus.

Kenny and Erin were hardly poster kids for unswerving faith. There was grief, irritation, subtle blame-shifting, and more than a few calls to church friends for help with conflict and impasses. Sometimes they just felt emotionally numb. Dreams for which they'd sacrificed had now collapsed, leaving debris around and within. Sometimes the burden felt almost intolerable. They'd never known this kind of weakness.

But as Kenny and Erin turned to God and others for help, they also experienced the unlikely grace of unexpected power. They experienced it in two ways: the power to stoop and the power of satisfaction.

### The Power to Stoop

Where is God when your largest assets become your greatest liabilities? Where do you turn when something that brought you excitement and elation becomes a source of deep, sharp, even insufferable pain? Large burdens enhance our experience of gravity—at least that's how it feels. We bend toward the ground. A head once swollen with achievement and exalted by success collapses under the weight of self-significance. We are humbled, and we stoop low.

Kenny felt it. He descended along this path involuntarily and with rolling pangs of anxiety. Yet he couldn't deny the paradox playing out. The lower Kenny stooped, the closer he felt to Christ. And he started to see things a little differently. Kenny began to see that his cocky confidence in his own abilities was not the solution, it was the problem. He began to wonder, "Why do I need everyone to see me as super-successful?"

Erin knew something was happening too. Kenny was talking less in small group, and his comments didn't carry the same bravado. No longer was he boasting about a victorious life. Then, one Sunday the pastor taught from 1 Corinthians about the kind of people God really uses: "God chose what is foolish in the world to shame the wise; God chose what is weak in the world to shame the strong" (1:27). Kenny was quieter than usual after church. Erin suspected the sermon had hit the mark. On the drive home, Kenny said, "You know, this may sound nuts, but I think humbling us was part of God's plan. Maybe God has rescued me from only depending on myself."

Erin smiled as she leaned her head back on the headrest: "Who would have ever known we had to fall so far to learn so much?"

### The Power of Satisfaction

Like scalpels, thorns slice deep. There's the incision, the blood, and the throbbing pain. Attempts at extraction cause tender wounds, all compliments of one thorn's jagged edge. Then comes the healing, and it takes time. For Kenny and Erin, this included coming to terms with their loss, picking up the broken pieces, and finding faith to slowly rebuild.

They learned to bear the regret, reject the shame, and adjust to new financial realities. But as they were faithful to talk, confess, pray together, and ask for help, they noticed a change in how they viewed what God had already provided them. When life was about strength, Kenny and Erin were rarely content with what they had. If they were honest, they would say it was actually much worse than a lack of contentment. They felt entitled to a certain quality of life, and they saw hardships and weaknesses as unnecessary intrusions, things to endure and find relief from as quickly as possible. Marriage existed in part to help each other survive the bad times so they could enjoy the good times.

Trouble was, their search for satisfaction never seemed to find its goal. In fact, the older they got, the higher their standards for satisfaction became. Then came their thorn, and what satisfied would never be the same.

The thorn united them. Kenny and Erin had never known sharp division in their marriage, but they also hadn't experienced sweet unity. Their worlds were siloed into their respective responsibilities, which they both worked hard to maintain. The family each knew their respective positions for the game, but nobody really felt like a team. Needing each other more helped them to appreciate each other better.

But it wasn't just that. Kenny and Erin's newfound position of weakness helped them to see God's many gifts with clearer eyes. And as they learned to lean on their Savior more than their circumstances, they felt less fearful of future calamities. A deeper faith ignited in them a fuller appreciation of their experience of salvation. They learned to live satisfied today—not because they have all they desire, but because in Christ they have received more than they deserve.

Kenny and Erin began to see that their circumstances don't need to change in order for them to be satisfied in life. Because of the amazing riches of Christ, they can be "content with weaknesses, insults, hardships, persecutions, and calamities," for when they are weak, then they are strong (2 Cor. 12:10).

## Weakness Means Sympathy: Jesus Gets Us!

Are you experiencing God's power in the midst of your thorns? Or are you getting smacked around by trials and temptations? Maybe Kenny and Erin's story hits close to home. Maybe you've even printed invites to your own pity party. It's one thing to talk about the power God makes available when we are weak. It's another thing to experience that power.

*How do we access God's strength when we're weak?*

Here's the good news. In Hebrews 4:15, the author writes, "For we do not have a high priest who is unable to sympathize with our weaknesses, but one who in every respect has been tempted as we are, yet without sin." We find access to God's power through the One who understands our thorns. The high priest we have is Jesus

> We find access
> to God's power
> through the One
> who understands
> our thorns.

Christ, relocated from heaven to become the sacrifice and mediator for his people.

Don't rush past this verse. Pause and ponder it. As our high priest, Jesus is not rigidly religious, gigantically judgmental, or dangerously disconnected from real life. Jesus is no Pharisee, rolling his eyes when we fail, outwardly tolerating us but inwardly reviling our weaknesses. No, Jesus actually sympathizes with us where we are weak.

Jesus knows you are weak, and *he gets you*. He doesn't merely listen well. He sympathizes. He understands the real frustrations you encounter. As a loving high priest, he empathizes with the areas in which you suffer. And he doesn't sympathize as an outsider. He's not the guy who read a book on weakness or quickly googled it to become conversant. No, the Savior knows you on an experiential level. As our perfect high priest, Jesus is "one who in every respect has been tempted as we are."

What defining moments of weakness are you facing right now? Bad week battling lust? Jesus understands. He knows the temptation. Struggling with resentful thoughts over some way you feel mistreated? Jesus gets it. He was royally shafted by people and wrestled through the temptation to feel resentful. Fretting over work? Sweating the finances? Feeling forgotten? Jesus knows all this. Tempted to throw in the towel, to give up on your role as husband or wife? Tempted to say you aren't cut out for this? Jesus understands that too. Concerning Christ's temptations, Raymond Brown writes:

> No one on earth, before or since, has ever been brought through such spiritual desolation and human anguish. For this reason, he can help us in our moments of temptation. He is aware of our needs because he has experienced to the full the pressures and testings of life in this godless world.[3]

3. Raymond Brown, *The Message of Hebrews*, The Bible Speaks Today (Downers Grove, IL: InterVarsity, 1982), 92.

Always remember: Jesus knows how a fallen world affects you, how temptations compete for supremacy within your soul. Jesus gets the shame—the demoralizing feeling that accompanies the skirmish between what you feel and who you are called to be.

Jesus understands, and he sympathizes with us. He's written our story. And from that place of perfect knowledge, dipping all the way down to our DNA, he issues this life-transforming invitation: "Let us then with confidence draw near to the throne of grace, that we may receive mercy and find grace to help in time of need" (Heb. 4:16).

Are you weak? Is your marriage seriously suffering? Are you in need of power when you're experiencing thorns? Draw near, Jesus says, and in the cleft of weakness you'll find his power.

*To make you strong and your marriage last long!*

# Defining Moment #3:
# The Moment of Weakness

We are weak. In fact, marriage is the union of two people on a journey to discover their weakness. But God sends weakness for our good. Thorn-constructed weakness creates the fruit necessary for marriages to go the distance.

| | The Moment | Our Response |
|---|---|---|
| **The Decision for Truth** | When I encounter my weakness and inability, will I persist in grief, irritation, and blame-shifting? | *Or* will I see life's thorns as gifts from Jesus? |
| **The Cost Required** | Will I persist in self-reliance, self-confidence, and self-sufficiency in spite of the weakness that marriage exposes? | *Or* will I believe that God has tailored a weakness for our marriage in order to make us more dependent upon him? |
| **The God-Exalting Opportunity** | Am I concerned that people are thinking too little of me? | *Or* am I concerned that people are thinking too much of me and too little of Jesus? |
| **The Way It Grows the Soul** | Will I set my attention and affections on what God has denied—an immediately discernable purpose in this weakness? | *Or* will I shift my gaze to what he supplies—a firm promise that when I am weak, he is strong? |
| **The Way It Sets Our Destination** | Will I refuse to be satisfied with life unless my circumstances change? | *Or* will I believe that in Christ I have already been given more than I deserve? Will I find in him—and in the strength he gives—the secret for being content (Phil. 4:12–13)? |

# STICKING T♥GETHER

DEFINING MOMENT #4:

# When You Realize Family Can't Replace Church

I'm not sure when I first noticed it. I think it was about eight years ago. At first I thought it was just me. Then I began to pay closer attention. I poked around online. Sure enough, it was true: *church attendance among Christians has slid from three times a month to twice a month.*

Now, I recognize this hardly qualifies as a discovery. It's nothing like Newton pondering falling apples and discovering gravity. But when you think about it, Newton noticed what was already there. He just got to thinking about why it happens. That's what I want to do with this chapter. Let's think about the dropping apple of modern-day church attendance and talk about what it really means.

But before we jump into the why behind the decline in church attendance, I want to raise an obvious question. Why are we talking about church attendance in a marriage book? That's easy to explain. Declining church attendance is only a symptom of a deeper problem. The deeper problem is that our family units, with all of their weekend expectations and commitments, are increasingly being prioritized over gathering with God's people.

Do you think that helps or haunts marriage? For me, the answer became a defining moment.

I was raised as a passive Presbyterian. Some of you may have enjoyed church experiences with more life or even a smattering of enthusiasm. But my roots were with Dutch and Eastern European Presbyterians, all of whom came from centuries-old hands-glued-in-pockets stock. If someone's arms were raised, it probably meant they were being robbed. I'm serious, the only time emotion surfaced was at the final "Amen." That meant church was done, and everyone's arms were liberated to eat the casseroles stacked deep throughout the fellowship hall.

While I was growing up in this context, the question of which institution took priority—the family or the church—was irrelevant. Church was something we did only occasionally, but we always attended on holidays so we wouldn't miss that blessing God threw our way every Easter and Christmas.

In college I was converted, got married, and joined a church where involvement meant we were living in community together. We loved going to church on Sunday because we anticipated seeing friends, hearing preaching, enjoying worship, and learning how to build our new marriage. The church became a priority in our lives and we loved it. Attending twice a month would've felt like we were leaving a Steelers game at halftime to go do something with our family. Now, family is important, but you just don't play hooky on the Steelers!

To be fair, and also appropriately circumspect, the decline in church attendance to twice a month is not the only way commitment to church has been downgraded. The rise of internet preaching, the growth of self-directed spirituality, lower bars for membership and commitment, and nonrelational church cultures must also be cited. But there's a specific reason I'm highlighting this new Christian tendency to elevate family over the church:

meaningful involvement in a gospel-preaching church links directly to having a durable marriage. Also, this question of whether families should be prioritized over gathering with God's people is not merely a duel between family-first advocates and church leaders trying to win back their market share. No, Jesus himself pushes forward the dilemma. He spoke to his culture, where the primacy of the family, much like in my buttoned-up Reformed upbringing, reigned undisputed.

## How God Feels about the Family

Before we take a look at Jesus's words, we need to understand the biblical context into which he spoke them. It's not just that Israel randomly happened to be pro-family in New Testament times. They got this idea from God himself.

God loves families. The family was his idea. Husbands, wives, marriages, kids—the whole lot—all spring from our Creator's love and blessing. God takes family so seriously that he installed "Honor your father and your mother" as the fifth of the Ten Commandments (Exod. 20:12), and he commanded faithfulness between husbands and wives in the seventh (Exod. 20:14). Solomon tells us, "Behold, children are a heritage from the LORD, the fruit of the womb a reward" (Ps. 127:3). Paul tells Timothy that "if anyone does not provide for his relatives, and especially for members of his household, he has denied the faith and is worse than an unbeliever" (1 Tim. 5:8).

> God is not simply pro-family. He invented family, and he's given it his highest blessing.

God is not simply pro-family. He invented family, and he's given it his highest blessing.

Then Jesus comes along and complicates things:

> Do not think that I have come to bring peace to the earth. I have not come to bring peace, but a sword. For I have come to *set a*

*man against his father, and a daughter against her mother, and a daughter-in-law against her mother-in-law. And a person's enemies will be those of his own household. Whoever loves father or mother more than me is not worthy of me, and whoever loves son or daughter more than me is not worthy of me.* And whoever does not take his cross and follow me is not worthy of me. Whoever finds his life will lose it, and whoever loses his life for my sake will find it. (Matt. 10:34–39, emphasis mine)

Jesus tells us that part of his mission is to bring division in families. How can this be? Is Jesus at odds with the Father?

A couple chapters later in Matthew's Gospel, we read an account that helps to illustrate what Jesus meant by his hard words. The Savior was teaching a large group of people when his mother and brothers arrived. They wanted to speak to Jesus, but they couldn't get near because of the crowd. Someone passed the request up the chain to Jesus. However, rather than stopping what he was doing and rolling with a family-comes-first attitude, Jesus replied, "'Who is my mother, and who are my brothers?' And stretching out his hand toward his disciples, he said, 'Here are my mother and my brothers! For whoever does the will of my Father in heaven is my brother and sister and mother'" (Matt. 12:48–50). Jesus shows us that his family of disciples takes priority even over his own mom!

You may already be thinking of ways to soften or explain away Matthew's record. But before you do, notice how Jesus ups the ante in the Gospel of Luke: "If anyone comes to me and does not *hate his own father and mother and wife and children and brothers and sisters*, yes, and even his own life, he cannot be my disciple" (Luke 14:26, emphasis mine). One can only imagine how that went over with the relatives. One author wrote:

While shocking to us, the meaning of Jesus's statement in Luke would have been especially challenging to his first-century audience. Ancient Mediterranean society was a strong-group culture.

The health and survival of the group took priority over the goals and desires of individual members. Loyalty to family constituted the most important relational virtue for persons in the New Testament world.[1]

The New Testament world would have agreed with our culture that biological and adoptive family relationships are vitally important in this life. But Jesus makes abundantly clear that these relationships must not be our first priority.

## Our New Family

I recently read that a really popular Christian author no longer attends church. When asked how he now finds intimacy with God, he said it comes from building his company. For him, God's church is a subjective concept that can be customized to fit his lifestyle. Church is private and personally adaptable. This is a Christianity that only winks at the Scriptures while caressing the culture.

The Western church loves private, personal stuff. We have *personal* Bible study, *personal* evangelism, and *personal* prayer— all designed to enhance our *personal* relationship with Christ. None of this is wrong. In fact, much of it is quite helpful. But our personal relationship with Christ is only a slice of the Christian experience.[2]

1. Joseph Hellerman, "Our Priorities Are Off When Family Is More Important Than Church," *Christianity Today*, August 4, 2016, https://www.christianitytoday .com/ct/2016/august-web-only/if-our-families-are-more-important-than-our -churches-we-nee.html.
2. Though a dated book, Gene A. Getz makes this same point in his classic *Praying for One Another* (Wheaton: Victor, 1982), 11. He writes,
   The hallmark of Western civilization has been rugged individualism. Because of our philosophy of life, we are used to the personal pronouns "I" and "my" and "me." We have not been taught to think in terms of "we" and "our" and "us." Consequently, we individualize many references to corporate experience in the New Testament, thus often emphasizing personal prayer. The facts are that more is said in the Book of Acts and the epistles about corporate prayer, corporate learning of biblical truth, corporate evangelism, and

A similarly subtle temptation for Christians is the idea that quality time with our families must be protected at all costs. Since parents often find their identity wrapped up in their kids' successes, cultivating their kids' extracurriculars—sports, academics, and hobbies—begins to take precedence over loving the church. And since we're regularly encouraged to pursue our spouse as part of our Christian duty (I've been nudging you in that direction in this book), we fight to invest in our marriage even when it sometimes means failing to love our neighbors or serve the believing community.

The Bible speaks against both our individualism and our family-first mentality. In fact, a key truth echoes down the corridors of both testaments: *our individual destiny is inseparably bound to our identity as part of God's people.*

In one of the earliest acts in God's redemption plan, he called Abram to leave his home and his family and go to the place God would show him. Why? God removed Abram from his family of birth in order to establish a new people through him—the family of faith (Gen. 12; Rom. 4). He had more in store for Abram—later Abraham—than building a temporary nation; he had a new eternal city in mind. As the author of Hebrews tells us:

> By faith Abraham obeyed when he was called to go out to a place that he was to receive as an inheritance. And he went out, not knowing where he was going. By faith he went to live in the land of promise, as in a foreign land, living in tents with Isaac and Jacob, heirs with him of the same promise. For he was looking forward to the city that has foundations, whose designer and builder is God. (Heb. 11:8–10)

---

corporate Christian maturity and growth than about the personal aspects of these Christian disciplines.

Accordingly, pastor John Onwuchekwa observes: "Prayer is mentioned no less than twenty-one times in Acts. . . . [T]hese prayers are inherently corporate. Whenever prayer is mentioned, it overwhelmingly involves others." John Onwuchekwa, *Prayer: How Praying Together Shapes the Church* (Wheaton: Crossway, 2018), 95.

Just like Abraham, God is calling us into greater eternal realities. "So then you are no longer strangers and aliens," Paul tells the Ephesians, "but you are fellow citizens with the saints and members of the household of God. . . . In him you also are being built together into a dwelling place for God by the Spirit" (Eph. 2:19, 22). Here's Paul's take: Christ purchased individuals to be members of God's household. Our personal autonomous life—and our earthly family-first life—has ended because we've been adopted into a new household by the uniting power of the new covenant. Our independence must be exchanged for membership in God's new family.

Sadly, some believers never shed their private, self-directed faith. As a result, an emphasis on individual or single-household fulfillment continues to overshadow the church's family identity. If left unchallenged, this imbalance creates lopsided believers who view the church as just another institution to meet their immediate family's needs—like a hospital or a local school. When we cling to this sort of radical independence, we have an orphaned faith—that is, a faith *without the eternal family*.

## Our Family and Eternity

Okay, I'm going to say it now, and I want you to think about it. Are you ready?

The whole idea of family, in the way we experience it on earth, is only temporary. There is a day coming when the concept of family will be swept up into a more glorious and satisfying arrangement. Don't let that make you nervous. What awaits us is far more magnificent.

One day the Sadducees tried to trick Jesus with a question about heaven. Jesus answered, "In the resurrection they neither marry nor are given in marriage, but are like angels in heaven" (Matt. 22:30). Jesus is not saying that because marriage isn't eternal, it's time to toss it on the trash heap. No, he's telling us that something even better awaits. In heaven there will be one glorious marriage between Christ and his bride, and that marriage will satisfy and complete every desire we've had for marriage on this earth.

In fact, the eternal marriage between Christ and the church is the very point for which marriage in this life exists. Marriage on earth is a picture of that eternal reality. It mirrors a higher purpose. Paul explains, "'Therefore a man shall leave his father and mother and hold fast to his wife, and the two shall become one flesh.' This mystery is profound, and I am saying that it refers to Christ and the church" (Eph. 5:31–32).

In glory you will experience delight that far outweighs what you've experienced here and now. If your spouse is there, it's hardly a stretch to think you'll experience heavenly delight in Christ along with your spouse—the one you've delighted in most in this life. Being in heaven with your spouse will not be glorious because you go on being their mate; being in heaven will be glorious because together you will behold face-to-face the One to whom your marriage pointed.

> Being in heaven will be glorious because together you will behold face-to-face the One to whom your marriage pointed.

In Pittsburgh, where I grew up, there is a beloved amusement park called Kennywood. Back in the day, yellow Kennywood signs all around the 'Burgh pointed in the direction of what we believed to be the ultimate amusement experience—cotton candy, caramel apples, delicious treats. Oh, and did I mention the roller coaster that would stop your heart and expel the candy you had just gobbled straight onto the coaster tracks? Throwing up at Kennywood was a rite of passage, something to boast about in English class on Monday.

The Kennywood signs pointed people in the direction of our deep desires for amusement park pleasure, but the signs were not the reality. Just imagine some poor kid sitting under a Kennywood sign, thinking that where he sat was all there was to Kennywood.

He'd be pretty misguided, wouldn't you say? The sign, of course, served another purpose. It pointed forward to something else—something that would fill that child with unexpected joys.

When sinners say "I do" in this life, they become signposts pointing to the relationship with the Bridegroom, Jesus Christ. Once we arrive in heaven, the signs are no longer necessary. They are caught up into something more amazing than any amusement park—the marriage of Christ and the church.

What's true of marriage is true of family. Earthly families will be swept up into a greater reality—the body of Christ. This is not to say our believing family members will become strangers in the new earth. "Do I know you? You look vaguely familiar. Were we friends on Facebook?" Rather, as Rob Plummer writes, "If our children stand beside us in eternity, it will not be as our children but as our blood-redeemed brothers and sisters."[3]

It's not so much that we lose our old family but that we gain a new family—a larger eternal one. Right now family serves an earthly purpose. But the day will come when it will be transformed into a glorious experience that is multiplied and magnified by the larger family to which we are united. As Randy Alcorn has said, "God usually doesn't replace his original creation, but when he does, he replaces it with something that is far better, never worse."[4]

Many people have horrible experiences with their families. If the whole concept of family calls to mind brokenness and pain, memories that elicit deep shame, or something from which you had to flee, please know that what God is preparing for you is not simply a family reboot. Rather, it's what family should have been all along—only more glorious. Your next home will be led by a

3. Robert L. Plummer, "Bring Them Up in the Discipline and Instruction of the Lord: Family Discipleship among the First Christians," in *Trained in the Fear of God: Family Ministry in Theological, Historical, and Practical Perspective*, ed. Randy Stinson and Timothy Paul Jones (Grand Rapids: Kregel, 2011), 50.

4. Randy Alcorn, *Heaven* (Wheaton: Tyndale, 2004), 337.

perfect Father and occupied by new brothers and sisters who have shed the scales of sin. There is a future awaiting you where the memories of grief will pass. My prayer is that the idea of having your broken family swept up into a new church family—even in this life—will be joyful news for you. And I pray that as you walk in community with God's people, you'll find hope in the Father of love, who longs to one day bring you into a new home where you will no longer know suffering or pain.

## Our Family Priorities

"Okay, Dave. You've got our attention. My family needs to make the church community a priority. But what does all this mean for my marriage?" This is the right question. Let me answer it in three ways.

### 1. For your marriage to last, you can't walk alone.

Where do you go for help when you and your spouse are in conflict? Where do you go when you both are discouraged and need prayer? Or how about in the happy times, when you have a free evening and want to spend it with others?

One way the enemy unravels a marriage is by isolating the husband and wife—from one another and from the Christian community. It's a familiar pattern with a predictable ending. A husband and wife are locked in conflict over some issue. There is little progress, and civility is tanking. After a day or two there's a knock at the door. Shame has arrived to inform you that real Christians don't act this way, struggle with this issue, say these things, or go to bed angry. Shame lies, of course, pushing us away from the church community rather than toward it. Only humble cries for help can banish shame and bring hope when you're hurting.

Since the church began on Pentecost, it has existed for community, care, prayer, mission, and growth (Acts 2:42–47). God loved us so much that he gave us this new family to ensure we are loved and served. One of the great benefits of being a part of a church is that God uses the church community to protect our marriages and to help them grow. That's one reason a lackadaisical attitude toward attending church is so dangerous. God never wants us to walk alone. Just listen to this exhortation: "And let us consider how to stir up one another to love and good works, not neglecting to meet together, as is the habit of some, but encouraging one another, and all the more as you see the Day drawing near" (Heb. 10:24–25).

Meeting to stir one another up to love and good works is an important part of why we gather. But the next line is amazing: "not neglecting to meet together, as is the habit of some." It's almost as if God inspired these words with our contemporary context in mind. God loves us even though he knows our propensity to drift from our commitment. He anticipates the temptation and calls us to avoid it.

How about you? How are you doing at meeting with God's people? Do you see it as essential to the future of your marriage? Do you make being with the people of God a priority?

> How about you? How are you doing at meeting with God's people? Do you see it as essential to the future of your marriage? Do you make being with the people of God a priority?

Sometimes we can neglect God's people in unthinking ways. You may buy a boat or a second home, and then you drift toward making these perks a priority on the weekend. Pretty soon it becomes a habit. But for your marriage to make it—for it to be supplied with what you need to go the distance—you must remain vitally involved in the local church.

### 2. For your marriage to last, you can't idolize the family.

God created marriage for our comfort, for our joy, and for procreation so that, when we are able, we might have children. God said to Adam and Eve, "Be fruitful and multiply and fill the earth and subdue it" (Gen. 1:28).

I'd be pretty clumsy if I didn't recognize that kids exert an understandable tax upon marriage. First, they arrive desperately needy. Then they enter school, and we become frantically busy. Then they become teenagers, and they become so desperately needy again.

And that's not to mention how kids impact our sex lives. When a young couple heads out on their honeymoon, they're thinking, "We get all the sex we want!" Then their sex life bears fruit and they have small kids. Soon their mantra is, "We get to have sex *when we have energy.*" Then their kids become teenagers, and they begin to cry, "We get to have sex *when we're not worrying about whether they're having sex!*" Then comes the empty nest: "We get to have sex when we want to, *but we don't want to quite as much.*"

God created the idea of raising children, and despite all the difficulties of parenthood, that fact alone makes our families seem like noble idols. These rascals, the high-minded idols such as family, are the most difficult to perceive. To challenge this idol is to come off as an anti-family, un-American, flag-burning opponent of what is sacrosanct to our way of life.

The challenge is that raising our kids can be so preoccupying that we don't realize its impact on our marriage until it's too late. When the kids come, husbands and wives can slowly drift apart. Our priorities—in some ways rightly—move toward our kids, and what they want and need takes center stage. If we're not careful, our marriage can become a mere apparatus to service our children's needs—a partnership to keep them moving forward.

Pretty soon the ground of our marriage is fraught with the weeds of worldly worries. We're consumed with what needs to happen for *our* children, and our thoughts for what God is doing for *his* family get completely choked out.

Earlier in this chapter I mentioned how we can let our kids' extracurricular activities take priority over being with God's people. I've noticed that involvement in sports takes a particular toll on a family's commitment to gather with the church. Weekend games and practices are more and more common today. And for gifted athletes who participate in travel ball, weekend games take a family away from their hometown and church multiple times each season.

Have you considered what the choices we make about athletics communicates to our kids about what's most important in our lives?

I've known parents who draw the line and say no to Sunday morning sports activities altogether; their goal is to cast a vision for their kids about the priority of God's Word and God's people over sports. As John Piper once observed, "There is a great gulf between the Christianity that wrestles with whether to worship at the cost of imprisonment and death, and the Christianity that wrestles with whether the kids should play soccer on Sunday morning."[5] Piper rightly sees our dangerous tendency to make idols out of our kids and their activities.

Yet there's an equal danger on the other end of the spectrum in the parents who make idols out of themselves and their leadership. Certainly, a godly father should provide loving leadership in his home. But there's such a thing as corrupted patriarchy, when unaccountable men use a few Scripture passages to unleash their selfishness and dominate their wives and kids. Even when the patriarchy is "soft"[6]—meaning it's tempered with gentleness—I fear it emphasizes fathering more than faith.

Families who follow this doctrine often feel life is good until one of the kids goes rogue. Only then is revealed the place where they've put their hope, and life falls apart because everything had been banking on parenting success.

It's no wonder so many divorces take place after the kids leave home. Whether through being child-centered, being patriarchal,

---

5. John Piper, *The Hidden Smile of God: The Fruit of Affliction in the Lives of John Bunyan, William Cowper, and David Brainerd* (Wheaton: Crossway, 2008), 164.
6. This sometimes happens under a distortion of complementarianism, but in my view biblical complementarianism doesn't require the baggage of patriarchy.

or by just being typical family-first Americans, moms and dads tend to leave it all on the field for their families. And when they do, there's nothing left for the marriage. It got sacrificed upon the altar of family success.

Husbands and wives, remember that one day your kids will leave. Live today preparing for that day. Don't skip your date nights for family time. Show your kids that Mom and Dad are a united front when conflict happens. Never tear one another down in front of the children. And make sure at every juncture that it's clear your relationship with one another—your marriage—is more important.

Oh, and take your kids to church too. In fact, explain why you do so. In this way you can build into them the truth that marriage is not an end either; it's God's people who are eternal.[7]

Dream with me for a second about what happens when a family is rightly connected to a local church. Imagine the transformational and enduring change that can happen as kids sit under God's Word, see adults worshiping the Savior, experience a history with a community of faith, watch their friends changed by God, observe how the gospel makes a difference in the lives of broken people. The best advertisement for a life of active church involvement is a catalog of memories where the gospel made a difference in and through the local church.

### 3. For your marriage to last, you must prioritize the church.

In 1 Corinthians 12, Paul writes to a local church about spiritual gifts: "To each is given the manifestation of the Spirit for the common good. For to one is given through the Spirit the utterance of wisdom, and to another the utterance of knowledge according to the same Spirit, to another faith by the same Spirit. . . . All

---

7. I love how one pastor put it: "When you wake up on Sunday morning and take your kids to church, you preach a sermon your kids will never forget." Jordan Easley (@JordanEasley), Twitter, July 10, 2016, https://twitter.com/jordaneasley /status/752123903791759360.

these are empowered by one and the same Spirit, who apportions to each one individually as he wills" (vv. 7–8, 11). The apostle is showing us the church as a body. We are each given gifts to edify and encourage one another when we gather. As parts of Christ's body, we are vitally connected to one another. "If one member suffers," Paul writes, "all suffer together; if one member is honored, all rejoice together" (1 Cor. 12:26).

What are the implications of this passage for marriage? The church is vital to marriage because each married couple *possesses* gifts. Not only that! The church is also vital because you and your spouse *need* the benefits that come to you as a direct result of others' gifts. If you are ambivalent about being with Christ's body, the other members of the body miss out on the blessing of your service. Moreover, you and your spouse miss out on the means of grace you can only encounter when you're participating in the fellowship of believers.

This is why praying together at night or sharing devotions together with your spouse, while commendable, is not the same as your consistent involvement in a local church. Never assume this is simply a choice for how to use your Sunday morning: "Shall we do breakfast, go on a day-trip, or go to church?" Consistent church-skipping may create family memories, but it also reinforces for your family what you most value. And your kids will pick up quickly that you believe the church is expendable. Don't be tempted to think, *We're just not needed at our church.* It's a lie. God has given you unique gifts for the building up of his body. For the sake of the church community, for the sake of your children, and for the sake of your own soul, don't withhold your presence from the body.

## A Higher Call

The goal of this chapter is not merely to change church's place in your ranking system or to boost your attendance on Sundays. If you're one of the two-times-a-month folks I talked about at the beginning, don't let me guilt you into clapping shut this book and declaring to your family, "It's now three times a month or DIE!"

No, my goal has been to speak first to the benefits that participation in Christ's body will bring to your marriage. Putting the right priority on the church will be a great grace to you and your spouse. Worshiping with God's people, confessing sin, listening to God's Word, and connecting deeply with friends—all of these graces are a supply system for your soul. So open wide the valve and keep it there. Your spouse will thank you. One day your kids will too.

# Defining Moment #4:
## When You Realize Family Can't Replace Church

Since the call of Abram, God has made clear that our individual destinies are inseparably bound to our corporate identity as a part of God's people. But it's still so tempting to adopt a family-first mentality instead of a kingdom-first mentality.

| | The Moment | Our Response |
|---|---|---|
| **The Decision for Truth** | Will I protect quality time with my family at all costs, pursuing and investing in my spouse and kids to the neglect of God's people? | *Or* will I see that when I make loving and serving God's people a priority, God uses the church to benefit our family in the process? |
| **The Cost Required** | Will I heed the siren call of the lake or the pool each weekend, feeling that I've earned the perks that come with personal fulfillment? | *Or* will I consider my responsibility to use my gifts and serve the church in love? |
| **The God-Exalting Opportunity** | Will I be tempted to think, "I'm just not needed at our church"? | *Or* will I remember that God has given me gifts to share with the church and that my family needs the means of grace that come to me as a direct result of others' gifts? |
| **The Way It Grows the Soul** | Will I focus only on my private, personal, and individualized relationship with God? | *Or* will I see that my personal relationship with Christ is only a slice of the Christian experience? |
| **The Way It Sets Our Destination** | Will I believe that my personal success as a spouse or parent, the success of my marriage, and the success of my kids are the most important things in life? | *Or* will I see that my individual destiny is inseparably bound to my corporate identity as a part of God's people? |

# CHAPTER
# 6

---

**DEFINING MOMENT #5:**

# When Your Spouse Suffers

I wish this chapter wasn't necessary. We need to talk about some difficult moments. Hard moments. Moments defined by the marks left, the tears shed, and the indescribable anguish at seeing the one you love suffer.

Marry someone and you're yoked to their well-being. Sure, we all bear wounds from our own battles, but marriage summons us to multiply the suffering. If your spouse is cut, you bleed. When they limp, you are weakened. Their diagnosis makes your knees buckle. Saying "I do" comes with unexpected crosses and undesired thorns. When your spouse suffers, a part of you dies.

Of course, it's hidden from plain sight when we sign the wedding license. The early parts of marriage are often spared these indignities. A young couple is magnetized by a love that pushes and pulls two individuals until they meld into one flesh. Then, like the early morning dew, one year evaporates quickly into the next. Anniversaries pass. Bodies age. Love becomes costlier. Age carries affliction. Yes, bearing our own suffering can deliver darkness and humiliation. But watching a spouse suffer brings sorrow that mere words cannot describe.

Lee understood. Or maybe he didn't. At the time, Lee's feelings were so complicated that his words lost their form. Where does one find a vocabulary for agony? Lee didn't know. All he knew was that he adored Georgia. Their twelve years of marriage were the happiest of his life.

An onlooker might have described their world as idyllic. Lee was the executive vice president of a local manufacturing firm. Sure, there were long days and respectable profits, but his greatest delight came from being a Christ-loving, churchgoing family man. Three beautiful daughters sprinkled sugar and spice and a frenzied touch of nice into Lee and Georgia's world. Family life ricocheted between sports, church life, friends, and the comforts of home. Lee's position and income afforded a nice house and other perks, including family travel. Honestly, it was the stuff of dreams. If life satisfaction was measured on a scale from one to ten, Lee lived at eleven.

Then it happened.

Affliction never knocks. It crashes the gate, uninvited. For Georgia, the crash came with a routine breast exam. "It's cancer," said the doctor. "And it's started to spread within you."

The next few years were a blur for the entire family. The cancer was aggressive, but Georgia responded with courageous optimism. For Lee, watching his wife suffer chilled his soul—like the frost on his windshield after a Wisconsin winter night. He wanted to help, to comfort; Lee wished he could even switch places and spare Georgia this misery. But there was little he could do.

Never in his life had Lee felt so powerless; he had never *been* so powerless.

Eventually, the doctors came to see that heavy artillery was the only hope. They would carpet-bomb the cancer through a bone marrow transplant. Replacing Georgia's bone marrow would bring her close to death, but the specialists reasoned that it would save her life. *Descend to death to save a life*, Lee thought. The ironies abounded. But it made sense. So Lee and Georgia gave the nod to the doctors.

The treatments worked, at least at first. Georgia improved and for a few years appeared to be beating the cancer. At year four, in fact, Georgia was declared cancer-free. Like a conquered enemy, the disease had been driven back and vanquished. Georgia was a survivor. Happy days followed as the gloomy clouds of fear and anxiety broke wide with rays of promise. For the first time in years, their future was bright!

But cancer can be treacherous, concealing its existence and mustering its forces in unforeseen places. A year later it unleashed an assault on Georgia's liver. The doctors concluded there was nothing to be done. After six years of battling this affliction, Georgia's body gave its last full measure. The Lord called and Georgia went home.

At the funeral, Lee stood speechless. He was a single dad with three girls—no wife, no mom—but still with a demanding job. He had a catalog of unanswered questions. The grief of watching Georgia suffer, of seeing her hopes raised and then dashed, of watching cancer slowly consume his soul mate . . . in the end, it just felt like they lost. She lost. He lost. The kids lost too. Georgia was gone, and Lee stood helpless before her grave.

> In this world your spouse will suffer. But how you respond to that unwelcome and unexpected suffering may be the difference between a cynical heart and a defining moment of hope.

By now you've realized this chapter covers suffering and affliction—but not in a conventional way. In this world your spouse will suffer. But how you respond to that unwelcome and unexpected suffering may be the difference between a cynical heart and a defining moment of hope.

## When Your Spouse Suffers, Where Are You?

Why does a spouse have to watch their best friend suffer? We've all heard sermons on suffering. They prepare, arm, and embolden us for dark valleys. But how do we prepare to watch the one we love suffer? I'm not just writing about the life-ending variety of suffering that Georgia experienced, either. How about panic attacks, migraine headaches, Crohn's disease, miscarriages, depression, or PTSD? Those are just a few of the hundreds of maladies that afflict the people we love.

When it comes to a suffering spouse, death at least ends the nightmare. But waking up each day to your spouse's ongoing suffering makes life seem cruel. Death at least gives one a shot at closure, but a suffering spouse bruises (unintentionally, of course) all who love them. Life becomes hard. It's a pretty random association, but I remember once sitting in a movie theater and hearing a weathered cowboy in an old Western say something about suffering that has stuck in my brain for forty years. "Dying ain't so hard for men like you and me," whispered the outlaw Josey Wales. "It's living that's hard."

Where are you when each day extends the affliction for the one you love? How do you offer hope when your spouse is grasping for meaning, at times grasping for their very life? Are you able to be purposefully present while living through the worst parts of "for better or worse"?

Certainly, there are foolish ways a spouse can respond to suffering. The Bible pulls no punches in telling some of those stories.

- *Like Adam, some spouses go passive.* Adam was passive as Eve bit hard, then he foolishly accepted the fruit, grubbing it down like a sleeve of Fig Newtons. No, this was not the suffering of chemo or walking canes. This was ground zero for where it all started. Tasting the fruit released indescribable misery and agony into the world. Like a tsunami, sin and suffering broke over creation unopposed. The woman chose disobedience while her husband chose inertia and then chose disobedience himself.

- Show me a husband or wife who moves rapidly toward the hiss of temptation and I'll show you a spouse who's unprepared for that moment. The fall reminds us that when one spouse experiences suffering due to sin, the other can stand passively and try to find someone to blame.
- *Like Job's wife, some spouses go cynical.* In response to her husband's extraordinary suffering, Job's wife offered memorable counsel: "Curse God and die" (Job 2:9). She tapped out and left the building. Honestly, can you blame her? We've all had bad times, but it's unlikely any of us has ever lost all our kids, all our earthly possessions, and our physical health due to a direct demonic attack. But it all happened to Job. And when it did, his wife's counsel was basically, "Give up on God and commit suicide." Job's wife reminds us that when suffering comes, some spouses totally despair.
- *Like Abram, some spouses go self-protective.* As they entered Egypt, Abram feared he would suffer if the Egyptians knew Sarai was his wife. So Abram told Sarai to lie and inform anyone who asked that she was his sister (Gen. 12:10–20). Figuring that Sarai was available, the pharaoh took her as his own wife. It's a sad moment when a biblical hero goes pimping out his wife to save his own hide. But Abram didn't think twice about swapping Sarai in exchange for his own life. He reminds us that when suffering comes, spouses can be selfish and reckless—even to the point of abuse.

These three biblical examples of how people located themselves in defining moments illustrate a hard truth. *How we respond when our spouse suffers says a lot about our understanding of marriage.*

Lee got it. He was determined to be present for Georgia, to become a voice of unqualified affection as long as she remained alive. He rearranged his job so he could make all her doctor visits.

When the chemo started, Georgia dropped weight, lost her energy, and finally shed her beautiful hair. Every now and then Georgia would catch a sideways glimpse of her frame in the mirror. She felt like an extraterrestrial character in a surreal sci-fi flick—trapped in a body that was scientifically altered to satisfy some strange script. Lee could almost see what she was thinking. He intentionally praised her new hairstyle, the trendy "thinning and falling to the floor" look. He assured Georgia that to him, her truest beauties were not only untouched but thoroughly enhanced.

And now Georgia was gone. Lee never saw himself as better than any of the biblical characters mentioned above. He had no halo or angel dust to make him saintlier. He wrestled at points with feeling alone, anxious, and afraid. But Lee was a guy who assumed his promises of "till death do us part" would be tested by fire. It's just simple logic: one spouse would ultimately suffer and die first. Lee had always assumed it would be him. Despite the rawness and reality of his agony, in some distinct but inexplicable way he felt honored by God's call to serve his spouse until she passed. To be there from the first "I do" until the final, heart-wrenching good-bye certainly brought grief, but Lee could now see that their wonderful marriage was bookended with beauty and closure.

## When Your Spouse Suffers, Who Are You?

Seeing a spouse suffer reveals how we define and embody love. Lee understood that love meant sacrificing himself to serve his suffering spouse. Georgia's suffering became, among other things, Lee's calling—and subsequently a defining moment for his life.

I'm inspired by his story, particularly because I've experienced my own defining moments—times where Kimm has needed me over these last thirty-seven years—and my response was, shall we say, less stellar. Maybe you can see yourself in some of my failures:

> Seeing a spouse suffer reveals how we define and embody love.

- There's *Dave the Diligent*. This Dave has some game highlights. He surprises himself with bursts of sympathy and
small gestures of love. The things that need to get done
are dutifully completed. The problem is that his job is
demanding. He has piles of responsibilities. Even though
his spouse is suffering, work distracts and competes for
priority. This Dave can be confounding. He checks in just
enough to satisfy the duty of serving, but he never truly
checks out of the office enough to provide what's really
needed to be present for a suffering spouse.

- Then there's *Dave the Martyr*. Kimm is suffering, and
Dave is working bravely to keep things going. Dave sees
himself as the silent servant, but one only needs to scratch
the surface and this Dave will drop oblique references
to his catalog of sacrifices. For this Dave, left hand and
right hand must always remain apprised of each other's
activity. Sure, it's subtle. Overt grabs for attention would
appear unseemly—as if Dave were making Kimm's suffering more about himself. But in reality that's exactly what
he's doing. He's parlaying her afflictions into a celebration
of himself. This Dave uses Kimm's suffering for his own
glory.

- Next there's *Dave at a Safe Distance*. This Dave stays at
home to serve. He waits on Kimm in commendable ways.
But there's a distance he maintains between himself and
his suffering spouse. I mean, who really knows how far
germs can jump? Dave's acts of service are designed,
in part, to keep him insulated from his wife's suffering.
Sure, the Bible says that a husband is to love his wife
"as Christ loved the church and gave himself up for her"
(Eph. 5:25). But Dave assumes strep throat was not in
view when the apostle Paul spoke to the original
hearers.

- How about *"Won't Let You Tell Your Story"* Dave? This Dave won't allow Kimm to tell her story of suffering without painting himself into the picture. Her suffering triggers some similar story from his personal history. Her attempts to share how she's doing are co-opted by Dave's instinct to relate all stories of suffering to times when he felt the same. Whether he realizes it or not, this Dave actually contributes more to Kimm's suffering. Her original affliction—now combined with his self-centered behavior—makes it increasingly difficult for Kimm to resist a growing impulse to slap some sense into him.

- Finally, there's *"Draw Up the Will"* Dave. This last Dave is present, serving, and attending Kimm in her affliction. But Kimm's rehabilitation is clouded with Dave's worries over every symptom. Whenever she acknowledges a pain, Dave googles it to discover what it really means. His fears, roaming freely over the wild prairie of internet information, are immediately conveyed to Kimm. With this Dave, sufferer and helper swap places as Kimm persuades him it may be premature to order the casket. This Dave's greatest danger is not the presence of his fear but the absence of his faith. He needs a faith big enough to get his eyes off of his worry and back on his wife's needs. Thankfully, Kimm is willing to forget her suffering long enough to talk Dave off the ledge and help him nail his feet to the ground of God's promises. Thank God Kimm is around to help Dave through her suffering.

What do these Daves share in common? Selfishness, fear, worry, self-protection, anxiety, unbelief, confusion, exaggeration, self-service, bewilderment, disquiet—all represent opportunities lost for the sake of a personal agenda. Have you met any of these guys? Maybe one stares at you in the mirror each morning.

Face it. There's nothing easy about serving a suffering spouse. Not when the helper is a sinner.

## When Your Spouse Suffers, What Should You Do?

So, practically speaking, what can we do when we see our spouse in affliction?

*First, step in.* Suffering people feel alone. Sometimes there's a temptation to believe no one can understand how they are feeling or what they are experiencing. Conversely, the person who wants to help their spouse often assumes they know exactly what the other person is feeling. In those moments, the words of James 1:19 will help you get traction: "Be quick to hear, slow to speak, slow to anger."

Job's three friends nailed it—until they opened their mouths. They deserved a standing ovation for Act I of their performance. They showed up, sat up, and said nothing: "They sat with him on the ground seven days and seven nights, and no one spoke a word to him, for they saw that his suffering was very great" (Job 2:13). God understands the importance of listening. That's why he calls us to pray (Phil. 4:6). Show up, sit down, and listen well. The point in this moment is not the poetry of your words; it's your presence.

Then, once the talking starts, ask some questions and listen to the answers. Sufferers don't often understand their circumstances, so they need to know you've heard their heart. Stepping in with questions enhances clarity and stokes your empathy. You might ask: How are you feeling? (Pretty basic, right?) What helps to alleviate your pain or suffering right now? How is your soul? How can I pray for you? Are you being tempted in any ways where I can help? Where is God alive to you right now? Where has God's Word offered hope to you lately?

Suffering is a window into the soul. Listening well helps you peer through the window to discover where pain is felt and faith is under attack.

*Second, trust God to use you.* Have you ever felt you are too inadequate to help your spouse when they suffer? Maybe you don't fully understand the scope of their pain or the nature of their affliction. Don't worry. You've just met the first qualification to being a helpful voice. God delights in using weak people. It's overconfident people like the Corinthians who prove problematic. Paul reminds them that an inexhaustible spring is promised for those who seek to comfort others:

> Blessed be the God and Father of our Lord Jesus Christ, the Father of mercies and God of all comfort, who comforts us in all our affliction, so that we may be able to comfort those who are in any affliction, with the comfort with which we ourselves are comforted by God. For as we share abundantly in Christ's sufferings, so through Christ we share abundantly in comfort too. If we are afflicted, it is for your comfort and salvation; and if we are comforted, it is for your comfort, which you experience when you patiently endure the same sufferings that we suffer. (2 Cor. 1:3–6)

Paul says they are able to "comfort those who are in any affliction" with the same comfort they've received from God. The Corinthian church is an unusual audience for this lesson. They saw themselves as markedly more mature and prepared for the complexities of life and leadership. But to Paul they were still in diapers (1 Cor. 3:1–4; 5:1). So we don't think about them as the ones Paul would talk to about comforting others.

As evidence of their immaturity, this church had believed lies, tolerated fools, followed impostors, boasted unashamedly, and ultimately betrayed Paul for hipper celebrity leaders. But Paul had a soft spot for these knuckleheads. The Corinthians' self-centeredness made it hard for them to know how to care for one another when they suffered.

And therein lies the touchpoint for caring for your suffering spouse.

As Paul comforted the Corinthians, he was able to draw on the comfort he'd already received. As Paul comforted the Corinthians, he did so from a place of experience. He was able to draw on God's comfort not simply for personal hope but for the purpose of passing it along. Remember what he said? "If we are afflicted, it is for your comfort and salvation; and if we are comforted, it is for your comfort, which you experience when you patiently endure the same sufferings that we suffer" (v. 6). God sometimes *gives us* affliction to supply comfort and compassion to other people. Are you taking this in? Is God suggesting that some of our afflictions have a larger purpose in view—helping others who suffer?

God is so serious about helping you care for your spouse that he arranged some past affliction for you. Do you remember what it was? Were you inexplicably ill? Did you struggle with depression, grapple with an unexpected loss, or have your sense of security fractured?

I remember when God pulled back this curtain for me. It felt like shifting gears without a clutch.

The Christian life is not just a "me and God" thing. He isn't after mere comfort consumers. We are called to be comfort *carriers*, a people who take the comfort we've received in affliction and pass it along to others, beginning with our spouse. God has prepared us for this moment "so that we may be able to comfort those who are in any affliction, with the comfort with which we ourselves are comforted by God" (v. 4).

*Third, remember the circles.* Do you recall the nested circles in the chapter on brokenness? A suffering spouse may bounce back and forth between the circles as they look for answers in their pain. Suffering magnifies all the influences over our lives—our fears, our upbringing, our genetic predispositions, even demonic influence. When a doctor whispers a diagnosis of cancer, the heart immediately struggles with fear, the enemy pounces with lies, and the affliction may uncover a genetic weakness. In the trauma of this news, all of the nested circles start to spin. Ultimately, the greatest service we can provide our spouse is to remind them of the largest circle—the God of Providence. His grace holds it all. He superintends every event and moves it forward for our good. Think about Lee. What should he have said to Georgia as she lay helpless under the power of cancer, wondering what would happen to her girls? What can be said to Lee when he wonders whether he can reorient his life and thinking enough to raise three daughters alone? Each suffering person processes their experience differently. Sometimes they ask logical questions; other times pain bends their reality and they lose their way.

You're there to help point them in the right direction. Ultimately, the greatest comfort a sufferer can receive is not horizontal ("I understand") but vertical ("God understands, and he is at work").

And God's understanding is not theoretical. He doesn't simply imagine what the impact might be or get secondhand information about side effects so he can react appropriately. He truly knows.

Sufferers often see God's role in their suffering as that of a potter: he creates the clay pitcher and then maybe breaks it. But a potter holds the hammer and never feels its blows. *Sufferers need to know that our crucified God is different.* In Christ he knows our pain, and that's what makes his providence so comforting. I'm reminded of this each time we sing William Cowper's classic hymn, "God Moves in a Mysterious Way":

> Ultimately, the greatest comfort a sufferer can receive is not horizontal ("I understand") but vertical ("God understands, and he is at work").

Ye fearful saints, fresh courage take;
The clouds ye so much dread
Are big with mercy and shall break
In blessings on your head.

*Fourth, share God's story.* God's story touches our suffering in the person of Jesus Christ. "The Father of mercies and God of all comfort" (2 Cor. 1:3) sent his Son to ensure his people would experience his enduring mercy and indestructible comfort not in theory but in personal and tangible ways. Christ took the sins we committed and accepted the punishment we deserved to offer a mercy we cannot comprehend.

If the good news stopped there, it would be spectacular. But there's more. God could have resolved the problem of sin without addressing the effects of sin and suffering that touch our daily lives. But he's too good for that. He comforts us *in* our affliction with a comfort available because of his own pain. Christ was unjustly accused, publicly shamed, horrendously beaten, horrifically crucified, and divinely forsaken on the cross. All comfort was removed from Christ so that we might be comforted—and be able to comfort one another.

Go back and read that last sentence again. It's really important. Someone you love may need it right now. If not, you may need it soon enough. A primal need among sufferers is to hear Christ's story—to know he has been there. He knows how we feel, and he is near. He has a plan. When the floods of distress and anxiety overwhelm, sharing God's story keeps us roped to the harbor instead of floating without a rudder.

There is a reflexive human instinct—deep in our DNA—to reach out for people when our souls are weighed down. This is the flesh-and-blood variety of comfort. You've felt it, and your spouse has too. We want to talk it through, find a sounding board, bare our heart, find someone—anyone—with whom we can share our burden. But for comfort to be durable and meaningful in an ultimate way, it must spring first from an eternal source: the God who loves, who comes, who suffers, who dies, who rises armed with grace and comfort to help the suffering soul.

And what a never-ending fount of comfort he is!

Not long ago, Kimm and I went to Wakulla Springs, the site of the longest underwater cave in the United States. This spring gushes over 200 to 300 million gallons of water per day. Pondering that stat promptly crashed my brain. It's an endless supply. And that's the same idea Paul conveys to the Corinthians. In our God, who has suffered for us and won resurrection comfort, we now have an endless supply.

If we want to help our spouse, we'll guide them not only to share their stories with us but also to meditate on God's story, the spring of never-ending comfort.

*Finally, look for God's opportunity.* A suffering spouse can turn us inward. It's understandable—their condition hits home, disrupts our rhythms and realities, and preoccupies us as we seek to find a new normal. In such times our world can easily become affliction-centered; we're constantly talking about "the problem," researching "the problem," and providing updates to others about "the problem."

Such conversations are essential, particularly on the front end of a trial when husband and wife must understand what's happening and take time to process. Too often, though, "the problem" consumes a growing amount of conversational space, and we turn inward as a couple. We begin living a life fixated on problem-solving, too easily forgetting the divine plan at work in our pain.

But trials are never barren. They arrive pregnant with unexpected opportunity. Is there a nurse going through a divorce at the doctor's office you frequent? Are people opening up to you about their fears after hearing of your spouse's affliction? Are you finding that your trial, or your spouse's condition, actually serves to soften people toward you? When a spouse suffers, a vital experience must be anticipated. God tucks extraordinary opportunities into the center of suffering.

My friend Scott lived in Canada with his wife, Jeannie, a delightful woman suffering from a chronic kidney disease. A few years back, Jeannie's condition seemed to improve enough to make a trip to the United States. On the inbound flight to Denver, however, Jeannie passed out and collapsed near the airplane galley. She needed urgent medical attention. Hours later the doctors informed Scott and Jeannie that her condition had rapidly deteriorated. This bad news was followed by a startling statement: Jeannie could not be moved. She could not fly. She could not return to Canada. She needed immediate care.

Stuck in Colorado, Scott and Jeannie just looked at one another. *This couldn't be happening.* Since they lived in Canada, they had no medical insurance in the States. To complicate things more, they still had a mortgage payment in Toronto, so their only housing option was to move into a relative's basement. Scott and Jeannie already bore the scars of hard times, though, and they knew God wraps his purposes in our pain. So as Jeannie began her treatments, together they waited on God.

In the third month of the trial, a couple of families who knew Scott had once pastored a church approached him to start a Bible study. He and Jeannie talked and both felt strongly that God was opening a door for Scott to serve in this way. Over the next few months, the Bible study grew. People experienced God in significant ways. The group participants began to ask, "Should this Bible study become a church plant?" In this place where crazy was the new normal, Scott and Jeannie thought, *Why not?* Why shouldn't a couple of Canadian refugees with no money but plenty of maladies plant a church in the layover city where their return flight abruptly ended?

> The dividing line between God's will and sheer lunacy is often drawn straight through our faith.

The dividing line between God's will and sheer lunacy is often drawn straight through our faith. Scott and Jeannie understood this. They knew their situation was like something out of a reality TV show, but they trusted God and started City Church. So they followed his lead.

Three months after launching, the new church was able to purchase the building where they met. Less than a year later, Scott and the other leaders installed a new lead pastor. Why? Because eighteen months after their unexpected layover, Jeannie was cleared to travel. Scott and Jeannie could go home.

Just imagine it. As they lugged their last suitcase out of the basement, Scott and Jeannie didn't just leave behind a crazy layover trial. They left behind a new church, new friends they'd grown to love, and a city where they had a defining moment. It's a lesson for us all. Amazing things can happen when we look beyond our suffering to see what God may be doing.

One last thing. When Scott told me this story, he wanted to clearly convey the most precious moment of the whole experience. On the night before City Church's first public meeting, Scott returned to their basement home where Jeannie had just found a Facebook post announcing the first church service. When he opened the door, he found his wife crying. And when he asked why, Jeannie, with tears streaming down her cheeks, said, "The only reason you're here is because I got sick. Because I got sick, there's a church starting tomorrow. If that's what it took, then it was worth it!"

If you're reading this and your spouse is suffering, or if you are the one afflicted right now, always remember: there are purposes and opportunities in suffering that we can't begin to understand on this side of eternity. For now, we need not comprehend them; we need only prepare for them.

Dear reader, is your spouse suffering right now? Look for God's opportunity!

## Lee and Life

Several years passed as Lee learned to navigate the world of widower and single parent. Grief knocked often, but Lee had a good church and a busy world. Eventually the clouds parted and bursts of sun broke through. The arrival of light coincided with an unexpected and delightful source of comfort. One Sunday, during an inauspicious church service, Lee met a woman named Rhonda. As time passed, Lee and Rhonda discovered they shared much in common. For starters, they had both lost spouses. But there was more. They were both single parents with kids at home. Both were professionals. And they both bore the emotional scars of constantly seeing an empty space at the family table.

Nothing was choreographed or arranged. Lee and Rhonda enjoyed each other and began to reorder their schedules to spend more time together. They talked about the past, their pain, and the amazing ways God had surprised them. It wasn't long before they were talking about the future as well—their future.

One year later, Lee and Rhonda were married. Rhonda's two boys moved into a new home with Lee's three girls. Welcome to *The Brady Bunch*, part 2.

God's ways are mysterious. Lee and Rhonda didn't meet until years after their spouses were gone. But both knew God's timing was perfect, and in those moments when it felt like all was lost, God was present to comfort them. Initially, their suffering tasted bitter, but God did a work through that suffering that ultimately allowed Lee and Rhonda to experience him as sweet.

It's been nineteen years since Lee and Rhonda walked the aisle and for a second time said "I do." The ensuing years have been filled with happiness as they grew to delight in the comfort of being together. However, we live in a broken world where suffering recedes but remains. This time it knocked for Lee.

Two years ago Lee began to exhibit some unforeseen symptoms. While on a cruise with Rhonda, he experienced difficulty lifting one of his legs to ascend a staircase. Oceans have been wobbling people's legs for thousands of years, so he thought little of it. But upon arriving home, the problem continued. In fact, it grew worse. The strength in Lee's legs deteriorated rapidly. Doctors were consulted and the diagnosis bounced between an autoimmune disorder and something much worse—ALS. Each diagnosis carried complications, but the latter preyed on their fears like hungry tigers roaming the Serengeti.

The following months were not encouraging.

First Lee limped. Next came the cane. He completed his physical therapy and endured a number of painful procedures. But things worsened and Lee eventually needed a walker. If there's no change, Lee suspects a wheelchair is just around the corner.

Rhonda laments the loss of her husband's mobility. Two of life's joys were traveling and hiking—each now made impossible by Lee's deteriorating condition. Rhonda serves Lee in heroic ways. She's a voice of encouragement in much the same way Lee was during Georgia's chemo. Rhonda recognizes a spiritual battle accompanies every physical affliction, so she is quick to remind him of God's goodness. They pray together, and they still enjoy opening their home to others.

From the brokenness of Rhonda's past, she gladly identifies with Lee's fears. As a man familiar with affliction, Lee does the same for Rhonda as she ponders the uncertain diagnosis hovering like an ominous cloud over his life. How long will they have together? It's unclear. But in a beautiful way they thank God for their past affliction. It has prepared them for present uncertainty and future glory.

In a broken world where we have no control over the arrival of bad news, 2 Corinthians 1 becomes a promise that makes all the difference. Tucked within this passage is a reminder that our spouse need never suffer alone. God comforts us in our afflictions. He has prepared us for this defining moment.

God's grace is sufficiently vast to equip us for every dark valley— for every trial that may tempt and afflict the one we love. It prepared Lee to care for Georgia as she passed, and it now strengthens Rhonda for the uncertainty of Lee's future. They face that future together, knowing God has comforted them and prepared them to comfort one another. And in that place, bearing scars from the past and bright hopes for tomorrow, they stand together, "Till death do us part."

# Defining Moment #5:
## When Your Spouse Suffers

When you marry someone, you're yoked to their well-being. Bearing our own suffering can deliver darkness and humiliation. But watching a spouse suffer multiplies our anguish.

| | The Moment | Our Response |
|---|---|---|
| **The Decision for Truth** | Will I respond to my spouse's suffering with determined self-protection, keeping their pain at a safe distance? | *Or* will I be present—listening, seeking to empathize, and showing compassion? |
| **The Cost Required** | Will I secretly point the finger at my spouse, blaming them for the costs their suffering imposes upon me? | *Or* will I recognize that our good God has ordained this season and my response to suffering will reveal my own heart? |
| **The God-Exalting Opportunity** | Will I let the inconvenience I feel about serving my suffering spouse leak out in my comments and attitude? | *Or* will I remember that in Christ, who suffered for us and received resurrection comfort himself, we have an endless supply of comfort? |
| **The Way It Grows the Soul** | Will I be a comfort consumer, occupied exclusively with my own hurts but blind to the suffering of others? | *Or* will I be a comfort carrier, taking the comfort I have received from God to others, beginning with my spouse? |
| **The Way It Sets Our Destination** | Will I respond with a cynical heart, giving in to total despair? | *Or* will I respond with a sublime hope, embracing God's comfort in my affliction so that I can in turn supply comfort and compassion to my spouse? |

DEFINING MOMENT #6:

# The Moment You "Get" Mercy

As inventions go, marriage is in a class of its own. Think about it. In marriage, two broken people become so connected that all the masks come off. All pretenses are dropped. We start to feel so comfortable with each other that eventually we're strutting around in our underwear—or, on good nights, in nothing at all.

But here's the flip side. As comfort levels increase, we also drop our guard, and our fallenness goes on full display. We see each other at our worst. Bad attitudes, bad habits, bad hair days, bad breath—there are certainly unattractive moments tucked between the sheets of matrimony. And as we get older, our bodies morph, grow, and go gray. Gravity, shall we say, takes over, and at times looking at your spouse may provide a lovely but less pleasant visual than the earlier 1.0 version you married. (Ladies, of course I'm only describing how men appear.)

And that's the point. Marriage, particularly an aging one, becomes an awakening to the mercy of God. A place of safety where we see each other as God sees us (as we are, without any masks) and where we learn to respond the way he does (with kindness and compassion). In this way, marriage becomes a sanctuary. For two people growing older together, it's a reprieve from the world, a place of refuge—a home where two sinners can dwell peaceably in the comfort of mercy.

Recently, I was reading how Jonathan and Sarah Edwards's marriage grew into their middle-age years. The biographer, Elizabeth D. Dodds, observed that Jonathan and Sarah's marriage was like that of a profound, enduring, and comfortable relationship:

> Enough has been said about the beauty of love in the middle years of life. By such a time in a marriage, the trying habits of one's partner have either been accepted or no longer noticed, while the precious aspects of the other have become so much part of the consciousness that they are like leaf prints stamped in stone. Memories, both of happy times and sorrows endured together, are glued into the marriage. The ties between the two people are further fixed by the many years of jokes shared and the common body of experiences. At this stage in a relationship, to come back to the comfortable presence of the other after being out among many people is to be rested and at home. All of this comes only after there has been a profound tie of love.[1]

One will not find a better description of mercy's impact. Mercy sees the other's trying habits but grows to accept or forget them. Mercy sees the sorrows endured as glue that bonds. Jokes are swapped and experiences treasured. Mercy makes returning to each other a homecoming.

But you may be thinking, *That's great, Dave, when you're a Puritan like Jonathan Edwards. His brain was bigger than my Buick, and his wife was probably dropped from Angels Academy right into the bosom of his home. That's not my life. We're not skipping off into the middle-age sunset together. We have baggage. There's*

1. Elizabeth D. Dodds, *Marriage to a Difficult Man: The Uncommon Union of Jonathan and Sarah Edwards* (Laurel, MS: Audubon Press, 2005), 137.

*anger, resentment, unexpected bills, unfulfilled promises, broken dreams, and bratty kids. How do we express mercy when our marriage demands so much and is still much less than we expected?*

## The Power of Mercy

Mercy doesn't give us everything we want. In fact, mercy doesn't give us anything at all. Mercy does a profound restraining work. It holds back from enforcing punishment even when we deserve it.

Jean Valjean, the protagonist of Victor Hugo's *Les Misérables*, understands the power of such mercy. Valjean is an ex-con, desperate and starving. Then, a saintly bishop by the name of Charles-François-Bienvenu Myriel opens his home for the night. Rather than receiving this act of mercy with gratitude, Valjean sees it as an opportunity to steal the bishop's silver. During the night, he swipes several silver plates and flees. But he doesn't get far. The local police arrest him and march him back to Monseigneur Myriel's home, where, according to local protocols, he's formally accused of the crime.

> Mercy sees the other's trying habits but grows to accept or forget them.

In that dramatic moment, Valjean's future hangs in the balance. This will be his second conviction for theft, and that means life in prison. But something truly astonishing happens. Upon seeing Valjean in custody, the bishop exclaims, "Ah, there you are . . . I am glad to see you. Why, I gave you the candlesticks too, which are also silver, and will fetch you 200 francs. Why did you not take them away with the rest of the plate?"[2]

The police look on suspiciously, but the bishop has a divine design. He not only decides to give Jean Valjean what he'd stolen, but then he adds the silver candlesticks—the most valuable items in the home! Valjean stands slack-jawed, staring incomprehensibly

2. Victor Hugo, *Les Misérables* (London, 1864), 36.

at this display of undeserved mercy and grace. In that moment a switch flips in his heart. This audacious kindness becomes a key to free him from a prison of bitterness.

That's what mercy does. It takes people capable of stealing silver—or bickering over bills and bank accounts—and enlarges their vision. It crucifies the claims of the kingdom of self and announces the new reign of a Savior.

The cross doesn't ignore or deny our sin. On the contrary, it stares courageously at our worst moments and, like Monseigneur Myriel, it says, "Your story doesn't end here. Mercy writes a new chapter!" Coming to grips with such great mercy changes us and seasons us to be merciful as well.

### The Practice of Mercy

Let's dive a little deeper. What exactly happens for a spouse to show mercy like Monseigneur Myriel? Five things come to mind.

*First, when I'm sinned against, mercy makes reconciliation my goal.* The incredible mercy I have received at the cross becomes the starting point for how I respond when my spouse sins against me. The gospel tamps down my outrage and sense of injustice. It reminds me daily that I've received an inexhaustible mercy, and so I must pass this mercy along—inexhaustibly.

This means that when someone sins against me—let's say, for instance, one who shares my bed—my goals have changed. I am not trying to convict her of sin, because the Holy Spirit will do that. I'm not trying to exact justice, since justice was satisfied at the cross. I should never condemn Kimm because I feel she hasn't met my standard for repentance. Rather, because Christ met God's standard, his righteousness has been credited to her (2 Cor. 5:21).

The gospel wakes me up each day with a pretty transformational reminder: *Because of Jesus, I didn't get what I deserved. So I won't hold my spouse hostage until she gets what (I think) she deserves.* I can retire my inner cop who is always working the beat, looking for crimes, and policing to make arrests. If I discuss problems or sins with Kimm, I won't be doing it for the sake of my satisfaction or vindication; I'll be doing it, I hope, for the sake of reconciliation and forgiveness. I've received incredible forgiveness, so my goal should be to forgive.

*Second, mercy means I look at you with compassion.* I no longer see you through your sins or mistakes. Sometimes we want to forgive, yet we retain the right to be suspicious. We accept our spouse's apology, but their record remains. Have you noticed it's far more enticing to be a record keeper than a forgiveness dispenser? That's because it's hard to give up the power record-keeping wields. We want to hold the trump card so that, should it become necessary, we can pull it out and remind the sinner of all they've done.

Steve says he's forgiven Sarah. He says it constantly, especially when bringing up all the ways she has sinned against him. Sarah has asked forgiveness, and Steve granted it, but only because it was the "Christian" thing to do. When Steve sees Sarah, he's reminded of her sin. Bringing it up is another way to punish her for it. Steve assumes he's a forgiver, but he's really just a resentful record keeper in Christian clothing.

Unlike us, God does not keep a record of wrongs (see Ps. 103:12; 130:3). Our sins are not encoded on heaven's hard drives for easy retrieval. God doesn't keep our sin on the broker's table to negotiate better behavior from us. As Psalm 103:10 says, "He does not deal with us according to our sins, nor repay us according to our iniquities." Rather, he forgives.

If this is how God responds to sin, we should respond this way too. When your spouse sins against you and asks for forgiveness, it's an opportunity to declare not only your forgiveness but also God's. It's an opportunity to say, "God does not see you through your sins and mistakes, and I won't either. God does not keep a record of your wrongs, and I won't either." This is more than simple kindness. It's costly mercy.

*Third, mercy means I accept your confession at face value.* It's unlikely I'll be able to forgive if I wait until the sinner really "gets it" and returns with a deeper, more sincere confession. Truth is, forgiveness is not a reaction to a perfect confession. It springs from a merciful heart already poised to forgive. My heart is prepared to forgive because I remember God has already forgiven all my sins—even those I struggle to confess.

The call to forgive doesn't depend on your spouse—or anyone, for that matter—initiating a confession. Mark 11:25 makes this clear: "And whenever you stand praying, forgive, if you have anything against anyone, so that your Father also who is in heaven may forgive you your trespasses." The idea that I won't have a posture of forgiveness until someone repents is typically just a spiritualized way of saying, "Pay for your sins!" (see Matt. 18:28). Remember, bitterness in married believers is often wrapped in more subtle pseudospiritual garb.

Moreover, there is no biblical warrant for judging the sincerity or humility of a person's confession. The more I make my forgiveness contingent upon the quality of the confession, the more I move away from true mercy. In Luke 17:3–4, Jesus says that if someone requests my forgiveness seven times in one day, I must forgive. For me, I'm tempted to tap out on the third or fourth time, assuming they should keep their mouth shut until they muster a little more clarity and sincerity. But that's the extraordinary and sometimes maddening thing about mercy: it doesn't keep score.

> That's the extraordinary and sometimes maddening thing about mercy: it doesn't keep score.

*Fourth, mercy embraces love, but it does not tolerate evil.* Mercy is quick to forgive, but it does not enable abusive or destructive behavior.

While there's no biblical warrant for judging the sincerity or humility of a confession, the Bible does distinguish between godly grief over sin and worldly grief over getting caught: "For godly grief produces a repentance that leads to salvation without regret, whereas worldly grief produces death" (2 Cor. 7:10). In 2 Corinthians 7, Paul is glad he stood his ground. He was bold and confrontational in sending the "sorrowful letter" to the Corinthian church, and it produced good fruit—real change that cleared them from further guilt (vv. 11–12).

Because mercy embraces love, it refuses to submit to ongoing evil. Nowhere is this more clearly seen than in cases of abuse. If you're married to someone who is abusing you physically or sexually, this is critically important to remember. The highest form of love is not quiet submission to abusive behavior but boldly exposing the evil for what it is. As incredibly frightening as it may be to go public and get help, this may be the only way to truly awaken the person imprisoned in abuse.

One thing is certain: a loving spouse never helps an abusive personality by appeasing them. In fact, some forms of entrenched selfishness feed off the very mercy and kindness you so selflessly display. Merciful love doesn't appease such behavior; it challenges the delusion that props it up. Winston Churchill once said, "An appeaser is one who feeds a crocodile, hoping it will eat him last." The appetites of crocodiles are never truly satisfied. If you are living with a croc, name the danger for what it is and call for help.

*Finally, mercy means that I'll be patient with your fallenness.* Mercy doesn't put up with evil, but, as with weakness, it's long-suffering.

Whenever sinners come together, weaknesses are revealed and frailty is put on full display. We experience one another's humanity, imperfections, and limitations—lights left on, doors left open, wrecked cars, and forgotten bills. In these situations, no one is necessarily sinning; we're just annoyingly weak.

When the kids were younger, I once took them to the mall. Now, going to a mall once is one too many times for me. But the kids liked malls and we wanted to spend some memorable time together. Little did I know how memorable it would become, because shortly after arriving I realized *my phone was missing.*

A missing phone requires immediate action. I called a family meeting and distributed assignments to each child. We divided the mall into a grid, and I dispatched each offspring to a different section to search for where I may have dropped it.

Marching to some weird lost-phone protocol in my mind, I headed off to security to report the missing phone in case it was handed over to lost and found. While I was there another thought surfaced: *Why drive all the way home—only to come back to the dreaded mall to buy another phone?* So I shuffled off to the phone store and purchased another phone.

You know where this is going, don't you? When we got home, my stupid phone was sitting on the counter.

How do you think a wife should play that?

Men always assume we know how to play that. We men are experts at seizing such moments for what a younger generation calls mansplaining: "Dear, haven't I told you this is why God invented purses with nifty pockets? It's like a kangaroo's pouch. You can store your phone right there!"

Women like Kimm are far more diplomatic. There was no teaching moment, no lectures, no subtle jabs at my forgetfulness. Only a laugh that could be heard throughout the neighborhood as she explained to the kids that this was God's way of ensuring men always had new phones. I had to laugh at myself. And as I considered Kimm's response, I discovered once again that in a moment of weakness I had encountered mercy.

These are defining moments. When they happen like this, they season a marriage. They help me see I don't need to be perfect. Being forgetful will not separate us. At a minimum, it will entertain my wife. And as we laugh, I am reminded of Paul's words to the weak: "And we urge you, brothers, admonish the idle, encourage the fainthearted, help the weak, be patient with them all" (1 Thess. 5:14).

Mercy's goal is reconciliation. Mercy looks with eyes of compassion. Mercy accepts confession. Mercy does not tolerate evil.

Mercy is patient. But what happens when we conveniently forget Paul's words about mercy?

## Without Mercy, I'm an Enforcer

Absent mercy, we will never see our spouse as anything more than a project or a pagan. Without mercy, marriage gets reduced to bickering about taxes and toilet seats until a new category— "irreconcilable differences"—mercilessly emerges.

Some who are reading this will be familiar with the unforgiving servant parable in Matthew 18:28. The man had just been forgiven an enormous debt, but when he encountered a fellow servant who owed him a smaller amount, he enforced the penalty for the lesser debt. The unforgiving servant assumed he had the right to take vengeance.

Here's the truth: every married person in history has been sinned against by their spouse. And when we're sinned against, we instinctively feel we have the right to assign blame and enforce a penalty. We assume our aggrieved status gives us the right to exact vengeance. We become punishers. Enforcers.

Thankfully, however, those moments don't need to define us. Why?

Because the cross relieves us of the need to enforce punishment. How? By leveling the playing field. The cross reminds us God has forgiven us an incomprehensible debt.

At the heart of the gospel is our own great injustice. But the One who truly is the enforcer—the Great Judge himself—chose not to enforce the penalty for our sins. Instead, he bore that penalty on the cross: "For our sake he made him to be sin who knew no sin, so that in him we might become the righteousness of God" (2 Cor. 5:21).

The only way to put down the enforcer mentality is by rehearsing this good news. Remembering you've been forgiven the greatest debt will set you free from the need to exact vengeance for the sins inflicted on you. Because we have received forgiveness, we can freely forgive.

## Without Mercy, I'm Irreconcilable

"Irreconcilable" is one of those words you can't just drop on folks without explaining. It means grudge-holding, unforgiving, and implacable. Think of it as a more sophisticated way to insulate bitterness. We create inner apologetics defending why we don't need to reconcile.

But it's dangerous—*very* dangerous.

Not long ago I was speaking with someone who felt I had sinned against him. In fact, I think he was right. I immediately confessed my sin and asked his forgiveness. But he said he couldn't forgive me because there was so much more sin for me to see. For him, my confession was not the budding of a grace worth celebrating but the weed to a sprawling root system. My entire sin complex needed to be unearthed and treated with the insecticide of his insights. Involving other counselors along the way didn't help, since they couldn't see the sweeping scope of my sin or agree it was a reason to remain unreconciled. He could not forgive me.

James says, "Confess your sins to one another" (James 5:16). Confession is beautiful and biblical, but what do we do when confession only deepens the divide? Far from moving us toward reconciliation, my confession only confirmed what he long suspected. My acknowledgment of one sin meant culpability for everything he'd accused me of. True reconciliation could only happen, in his view, if I owned the entire list of sins he ascribed to me. And for this dear soul, that list had been long pondered and was dizzying in its details. So he's unwilling to reconcile.

What do you do when someone, perhaps even your spouse, marks your motives as irredeemable and refuses to make amends? When they are irreconcilable? Maybe this is a real question for you or for someone you're trying to help right now. How does

God meet a spouse or a former friend who has been sentenced to relational Siberia because of a grudge?

We tend to think in terms of "fixing" the problem by more conversations, owning what we can, repeating our perspective, and hearing from the other party. We can do this ad nauseam with hopes of the other party coming to agree fully with our perspective. Yet some people have a stubborn tendency to withhold forgiveness until their spouse (or whoever the alleged perpetrator may be) fully endorses their view of events.

The apostle Paul takes a different tack. Let's explore two passages that give us his perspective.

> What do you do when someone, perhaps even your spouse, marks your motives as irredeemable and refuses to make amends?

First, in 2 Timothy 3:1–9, the apostle gives a list of the various ungodly people who will roam the world in the last days. One word identifies those who are "corrupted in mind and disqualified regarding the faith" (3:8). The Greek word *aspondos* is used in verse 3, and simply put, it describes those unwilling to reconcile. One who is "implacable" (NRSV), "unappeasable" (ESV), "irreconcilable" (NASB), or "unforgiving" (NIV). The word speaks of a "hostility that admits of no truce."[3] This is a person—husband, wife, friend, or enemy—who claims to be a Christian but resists efforts to reconcile and contends they are obeying God as they do so. In other words, in this area of life, this person is acting like an unbeliever or a hypocrite who isn't listening to Jesus because he can only hear himself.

Here's a different twist. In 2 Corinthians 2:5–11, a man sinned in a serious way. This sinner repented sincerely, but the church would not accept his repentance. So Paul stepped in to make an appeal on behalf of this man. He says this repentant sinner is on the verge of being overwhelmed. In response, the Corinthian church should "reaffirm

---

3. Donald Guthrie, *The Pastoral Epistles*, Tyndale New Testament Commentaries (Grand Rapids: Eerdmans, 1990), 174–75.

your love for him" (v. 8). They should forgive this man even as he has requested. All of this must be done "so that we would not be outwitted by Satan; for we are not ignorant of his designs" (v. 11).

According to this passage, one evil device of the enemy—one scheme he employs—is to convince believers they don't need to respond to repentant sinners with forgiveness. And the sticking issue becomes *our* estimation of the offending party's confession. We assume the other party is just not genuine; we suspect they haven't yet achieved true metrics for authentic repentance. We block reconciliation by assuming we can X-ray their heart and discern its insincerity.

Mark and Shelly are offended because their friends hurt them. When these friends suggest getting together to discuss what happened, Mark and Shelly keep the door shut. They customarily go through the gestures of forgiveness and accept the apology, but the story of what took place isn't up for discussion. This story, sadly, allows them to remain victimized and unreconciled, even while they claim they've forgiven their friends. Mark and Shelly have constructed a way to deal with hurts that says, "I forgive you, but we can never be friends again." For them, forgiveness does not mean reconciliation. It's a protection from, not a restoration of, relationship.

Yes, there are situations where we must distinguish between forgiveness and relationship, forgiveness and trust, or forgiveness and reconciliation. An abused wife may forgive her husband, but that doesn't mean she's obligated to immediately return home. Trust must be restored first. A business executive can forgive a staff member who embezzled money, but that forgiveness does not protect the embezzler's job. They are forgiven and fired. Why? Forgiveness is present but trust is not. In such cases, true mercy forgives and acts wisely. It does not place abusers or embezzlers back into situations for which they are unprepared or into relationships where there hasn't been enough time for trust to be re-earned.

These are important distinctions, but they are the exception. Twisting the Scriptures to remain unreconciled is more common. And it's getting worse as each year passes. Each time we play the "irreconcilable" card, we overlook the words of our Savior: "Pay attention to yourselves! If your brother sins, rebuke him, and if he repents, forgive him, and if he sins against you seven times in the day, and turns to you seven times, saying, 'I repent,' you must forgive him" (Luke 17:3–4).

Confessing seven times a day hardly even seems like repentance. But it's not our job to parse the souls of others and judge the quality of their confessions. Our job is to maintain a heart that is quick to respond to sincere confessions and anticipates good fruit from the lives of repentant people. Wise is the couple who errs on the side of forgiving rather than risking the rapid spiritual decay of *aspondos*! I think that's why Jesus opened the passage by saying, "Pay attention to yourselves!" Richard Baxter described the magnitude of Christ's forgiveness this way:

> Jesus Christ came to pardon sin and cover the infirmities of his servants, and to cast them behind his back into the depth of the sea and to bury them in his grave. It is the censurer's work to rake them up and to bring them into the open light.[4]

If you're reading this section and coming to see that you are censuring your spouse, raking up their sins again and again because they've really hurt you, remember the distinction already drawn: *Forgiveness is freely given; trust requires time.* A true heart of forgiveness opens up opportunities for trust. It doesn't shut out the sinner due to lack of trust.

> Forgiveness
> is freely
> given; trust
> requires time.

How do you respond when you are sinned against? The way we answer this key question is really important. In fact, I'd go one step further. *How we respond to sin reveals our true grasp of the gospel.*

4. Richard Baxter, *A Christian Directory, Part IV: Christian Politics*, section 24.3.7, in *The Practical Works of Richard Baxter: with a Preface, Giving Some Account of the Author, and of this Edition of His Practical Works: An Essay on His Genius, Works and Times: and a Portrait*, vol. 1 (London, 1838), 864.

## Mercy for the Weary Spouse

Perhaps the greatest threat to mercy is not our becoming an enforcer or being irreconcilable but simply growing tired. There is a corrosive fatigue that emerges when I begin to grow weary of my spouse's fallenness. How about you? Are you weary of the sins of another? Or exhausted at being unforgiven by a spouse? John Calvin says, "[Christ] expressly declares that there ought to be no limit to forgiving; for he did not intend to lay down a fixed number [of times to forgive], but rather to enjoin us never to become wearied."[5]

I have to wonder if it was weariness that contributed to the attitude of the unforgiving servant. Perhaps he simply got tired of having someone in his debt. He forgot what he should have remembered (that he had been forgiven a great debt) and remembered what he should have forgotten (that he had a smaller debt owed him).

Our spouse's weakness can be significant, and change can be slow, sometimes even indiscernable. The husband may never get comfortable sharing his feelings in a way that fully satisfies the wife. The wife may never display the same capacity as the husband in running that particularly bothersome part of the home. Without mercy for weakness, those mundane areas where change inches along can become miles of resentment.

You know you're growing weary when you start to feel like, "Lord, why did you give me *him* with all that baggage or *her* with all those limitations?"

The call here is not to suck it up and just endure your spouse. The answer is to stare once again at the debt you have been forgiven. Be freshly inspired by God's patience, forbearance, and goodness. Then, as Paul writes to the Colossians:

> Put on then, as God's chosen ones, holy and beloved, compassionate hearts, kindness, humility, meekness, and patience, bearing

5. John Calvin, *A Commentary on the Harmony of the Evangelists, Matthew, Mark, and Luke*, trans. William Pringle (Edinburgh, 1865), 364.

with one another and, if one has a complaint against another, forgiving each other; as the Lord has forgiven you, so you also must forgive. And above all these put on love, which binds everything together in perfect harmony. (Col. 3:12–14)

Such mercy is beautiful because it seats two people across from each other to say, "My love for you will never be conditioned on change in your area of weakness. God has been patient with me. I'm called to be patient with you!"

In the classic *Moby Dick*, Herman Melville invites us into the mind of Queequeg. He's an idol worshiper who spends a full day in fasting and humiliation before his little god Yojo. Writing from Ishmael's point of view, Melville describes the wearying absurdity of Queequeg's Ramadan and Ishmael's quiet mercy as he restrained himself from giving the idolater a rebuke. But one line stood out to me as particularly insightful: "Heaven have mercy on us all—Presbyterians and Pagans alike—for we are all somehow dreadfully cracked about the head, and sadly need mending."[6]

It's an undeniable truth. The only question is whether we know it or not. For those cracked about the head who need the mending of mercy, there is wonderful news. We have it in Christ. And now, through him, we pass mercy along.

Do you see the role of mercy in the longevity of your marriage? Maybe you're thinking, *Dave, I've heard it all before. I've overlooked sin until it pollutes every part of our home. Mercy has been tried and found wanting. It just doesn't work!*

Recently, I was reading a book by Andy Crouch when I encountered a striking quote. His observation, aimed at social institutions, has undeniable application for the institution of marriage as well:

It is amazing how consistently the stories of even the most complex institutions come down to their trustees, the ones who, at their best, bear the institution's pain and brokenness, forgive it and serve it.

6. Herman Melville, *Moby Dick* (Boston: St. Botolph Society, 1922), 82.

It is amazing how consistently the fate of institutions hinges on a few people, and their own personal character, *how much even one person can tip the balance toward devastating injustice or toward redeeming abundance.* And it is amazing how often the most trustworthy trustees are those who have personally experienced the worst that idolatry and injustice can do.[7]

Are you a trustworthy trustee of your marriage, bearing its pain and brokenness while forgiving and serving your spouse? Or are you more of a complaining consumer, keeping a record of all the ways the institution is not meeting your needs? In Colossians 3, we are called to be merciful trustees, resolutely importing into the institution the gift we have freely received. "Forgiving each other; as the Lord has forgiven you, so you also must forgive" (v. 13).

Remember, one spouse with the courage to display God's remarkable mercy can "tip the balance . . . toward redeeming abundance" in marriage. Stop for a second and think about it. *That spouse could be you.* The adventure toward tipping the balance could begin today, even right now.

Christ has given us mercy so that it might be shared. And for those who can kiss a sinner good-night despite being sinned against, marriage becomes resilient—a durable institution. Because eventually they wake up transformed into trustees over a gift more valuable than they ever dared imagine. A union dazzling with the good news of what really happens when mercy triumphs over judgment.

---

7. Andy Crouch, *Playing God: Redeeming the Gift of Power* (Downers Grove, IL: InterVarsity, 2013), 219–20, emphasis added.

# Defining Moment #6:
## The Moment You "Get" Mercy

Every married person in history has been sinned against by their spouse. When we're sinned against, we instinctively feel we have the right to assign blame and then enforce a penalty. But there's a different option in those moments. Because God has shown us great mercy, we can show mercy to our spouse.

| | The Moment | Our Response |
|---|---|---|
| **The Decision for Truth** | When my spouse sins against me, will I feel the need to convict them of sin or exact justice for what they've done? | *Or* will I allow the gospel to tamp down my outrage and sense of injustice, reminding myself of the inexhaustible mercy I've received so that I pass this mercy along? |
| **The Cost Required** | When my spouse sins against me, will I keep a record of wrongs? | *Or* will I bear the cost of forgiveness? |
| **The God-Exalting Opportunity** | Will I enable my spouse's abusive or destructive behavior? | *Or* will I call out worldly sorrow and see that the highest form of love is not to put up with physical or sexual abuse but to expose its evil? |
| **The Way It Grows the Soul** | When I experience my spouse's weakness, will I lecture them? | *Or* will I have patience with and a sense of humor about their failings? |
| **The Way It Sets Our Destination** | Will I see my spouse as nothing more than a project or a pagan? Will my marriage be reduced to bickering about our irreconcilable differences? | *Or* will I see the role of mercy in the longevity of our marriage? |

## DEFINING MOMENT #7:

# When You Discover Sex
# Changes with Age

The guy was perched atop a stool at a counter in Starbucks. He was over seventy years old. His counselor—almost certainly a pastor—was seated next to him, speaking in whispered tones. But the guy was definitely not whispering. And here's what made it even more awkward. The conversation was *unquestionably* about sex.

For the record, if eavesdropping is *secretly* listening in to a conversation, I am guiltless. Along with the rest of the Starbucks clientele, I was *openly* listening. God bless this dear soul. Somehow he'd lived for seven decades and still not found the volume control on his tongue. I'm sure you've met this guy or someone like him. They talk in a sort of reality-distortion bubble, unaware that their normal conversation voice can fill every habitable inch of a city block. Put a phone in their hand and it practically gives them a superpower—the ability to seize everyone's attention within a square mile and then squash their conversation. Spiritually speaking, it's the gift of being a nuisance.

"We exchanged vows!" he seethed, slapping the counter for emphasis. "She has an obligation to deliver what I need. Once a day is not too much!" The counselor was trying to quiet him, but this man was unshushable. And he was just getting started. "I shouldn't have to live this way. This is a divorceable offense!"

Listening was a conflicting experience. Part of me was grieved over the way this man was twisting his marriage vows in a naked display of self-centeredness. As they say in the old country, what he was missing was a lot. Another part of me just wanted to tap him on the shoulder for details. "Pardon me, but seriously, you're seventy years old and you want sex once per day . . . *what kind of vitamins do you take?*"

The best part of me saw the bigger picture. One needn't be a prophet to see that the problems for this couple went beyond sexual frequency. Their issues weren't really about vows, libido, frigidity, or marital duty. And yet, Mr. Once-a-Day wasn't all that dissimilar from most married people. Whether husband or wife, young or old, rich or poor, healthy or infirm, we can all relate to the desire to have a sex life different from the one we are experiencing.

Why is this the case? What would you say if you were that counselor in Starbucks? (Besides *Please, for the love of everything decent in this world, lower your voice.*) And would it change if the man were younger, perhaps in his thirties, forties, fifties, or sixties? I know it's probably difficult for newlywed readers to understand, because right now it's impossible to tear some of you apart. But there are significant shifts that accompany aging and make sex more delicate and difficult. If one lives long enough, sex may be confined to cherished memories. Discovering these changes—which may include the end of your sex life—is a defining moment.

Our willingness to adapt our sexual expectations to life's changes reveals something about our soul. But what is our standard for changing expectations? Honestly, the Bible is relatively silent on the subject of sex and aging. So where do we start? Platitudes won't do. Sex is too intimate and important to be reduced to triviality. In that moment when we realize that sex in the future may be different from sex in the past, how should we feel? Relieved? Violated? Grieved? Plagued by sentimental longing?

If you'll allow me, I'd like to pass along some things I've learned from my years of studying, from counseling and asking others, and from being married for close to four decades. Let's rather unceremoniously dub this information "The Wise Soul and Aging Sex." But first, let me say a word about the format of this chapter.

> Our willingness to adapt our sexual expectations to life's changes reveals something about our soul.

After each main point, I've included a section called Wise Talk, where I offer some simple suggestions for how you and your spouse can discuss the material. Why? Because wisdom is useless until it's applied. And let's be honest, sex is far easier to read or think about than to talk about. Marriage is an adventure in oneness, and oneness requires communication. It may feel awkward to start, but God meets couples in profound ways when they open their souls to discuss the things that really matter. So bear with me and try it. Then see what God does!

## The Wise Soul Knows . . . Sex Is a Part, Not the Whole

Just so our terms are clear, real intimacy need not include sex. In a fallen world, and especially in an age of expressive individualism, our sinful cravings instinctively move sex to the center. For the believer, though, intimacy is not equivalent to sex. Rather, it's helped along by sex in much the same way my cell phone is helped when a new cell tower goes up. Thanks to my present cellular carrier, living in Florida means living each day with a low signal. This hardly qualifies as an affliction, but it does weaken my connection to other people. A new cell tower in the right location makes the connection strong. Sex is a new cell tower for intimacy. It takes our sense of tender affection and boosts it through the shared delight of husband and wife. Yes, people can live without their cell strength at five bars, and some married couples are forced to live without sex entirely. But getting the boost is rather sweet.

Marriage is more than sex. Way more. But as fringe benefits go, sex is pretty dope. It's not hard to understand why a sex-starved marriage would encounter difficulties. I think that's why Paul is so direct with the Corinthian couples: "Do not deprive one another," he exhorts (1 Cor. 7:5). He makes it simple: "The husband should give to his wife her conjugal rights, and likewise the wife to her husband" (7:3). Apparently, sex is so essential to healthy marriages that God didn't hesitate to use a single man to remind us. Important? Absolutely. But is a breathless sex life synonymous with a healthy marriage? Not by a long shot.

The sum of our marriage is greater than the use of our parts.

> The sum of our marriage is greater than the use of our parts.

That's not just a clever statement. Even among godly Christian couples, sex has a way of sliding to the center and making the part (or the parts) seem like the whole. It happens when sex is great, and it happens when sex is broken and in need of repair. A period of abstinence hardly makes us think less about sex. During a hurricane last year, our water was shut off for days. We learned immediately that the shutdown of something essential basically moves it to the middle of one's attention. Hardly an hour passed when we weren't thinking about water—dreaming about hot showers, running spigots, and fresh ice—all because our water was shut down.

I remember having a rather poignant conversation with a man in his late sixties. In a very humble, honest, and intelligent manner, he described the slowing of his sex life and some of the ways God was meeting them as a couple. The conversation took place at the end of a seminar as people were milling about, so I took the opportunity to ask, "What would you want to tell the younger married people in this room about how to prepare for what you are experiencing?" I'll paraphrase his response: "Don't reduce cleaving to sex. Make sure your sexuality includes communication, intimacy, and affection. Because the day may come where sex moves to the side. What remains are the other things you valued."

My friends, many of us just don't realize how many couples live with incredible frustration because they desire consistent sex with their spouse, but something is wrong. Maybe a hurricane has hit their relationship, or maybe the plumbing just isn't working right. Sex is delicate and easily disruptable.

How many spouses, for understandable reasons such as hormonal and physical changes, past abuse, or recent infidelity, have difficulty being responsive to sexual initiative or feeling sexually attractive? It's the paradox of sex. When it's going great, we think about it a lot and want to protect the supply line. When it's not, it's like the struggling child in the family who dominates our attention because they're doing poorly. I guess the point I'm making is that in almost every season of life, sex has a way of sneaking to the center.

## WISE TALK

Wise talk considers the past. The past has a powerful influence on how we think about sex in the present. It often shapes the role sex plays within the marriage. Can you identify any positive ways the past has influenced how you think about sex? God often surprises us with hidden delights in the bedroom. Can you describe for your spouse a specific way God has surprised you? Let's also flip it over. Are there any ways the past has obscured the place of healthy sexuality? What bad fruit can you locate? Don't be afraid to stare brokenness in the face. God is bigger and grace rushes at us when we open our souls in such intimate ways. Go to God together. He is there and poised to bless your humble steps toward him (James 4:6).

## The Wise Soul Knows . . . There Is No Normal

Forget normal. It doesn't help. This is not to make a case for abnormal sex, whatever that may be, or to set our expectations on extraordinary earthquakes of orgasm that constantly spike higher on the Richter scale. I'm simply saying there's no normal situation. "Normal" defines what typically happens. It addresses what is standard or customary. But if you imagine there's something normal or normative about the sex life of a lasting marriage, you have smuggled in a couple of unhelpful assumptions.

*First, assuming there is a "normal" establishes standards outside the realities of your specific marriage.* Not all assumptions are bad. For instance, as a general rule for premarital counseling, it's good to know men warm up to sex more quickly than women. But sex flashes from a convergence of factors that fluctuate with age. Our bodies change. Our desires change. Our chemistry changes. Our health changes. Our environment changes. Our needs change. Our resilience changes. And our energy definitely changes. To run strong, couples have to anticipate these changes together and mark them as God's invitation to define "normal" in a way that suits and serves their particular marriage.

> To run strong, couples have to anticipate changes together and mark them as God's invitation to define "normal" in a way that suits and serves their particular marriage.

Panting, passionate sex into old age is not a scriptural promise . . . or perhaps even a reasonable expectation. Regardless of what the studies say, sexual success cannot be defined outside of the individuals within a particular marriage. As one author observed, "Christians should recognize that 'scientists' with clipboards who watch other people have sex do not really have a firm grasp of what *normal* means."[1]

*Second, the idea of "normal" creates unnecessary expectations within the marriage.* The phrase "Most people at our age

1. Douglas Wilson, *Reforming Marriage* (Moscow, ID: Canon Press, 1995), 83.

or stage are doing . . ." can become a tool for condemnation, a club we swing for our own selfish benefit. That older gentleman I wrote about at the beginning of this chapter, who was beating on the Starbucks counter and demanding daily sex, was likely operating out of some self-serving vision of what's normal. Expectations conceived somewhere along the way remained unsatisfied, revealing a heart that loved the sex act more than he loved his wife. Next thing you know, his demanding heart is holding court in a coffee shop. Had his wife been there, I'm sure she would've had a different story to tell.

> Sex will never be pleasurable or durable when it's driven by the demands of one instead of the enjoyment of two.

When expectations drive our physical relationship in marriage, intimacy evaporates. Appearing in its place are guilt and shame ("I'm not doing what I should be doing") or anger ("My spouse isn't doing what *they* should be doing!"). Sex will never be pleasurable or durable when it's driven by the demands of one instead of the enjoyment of two.

## WISE TALK

Normal can't be prescribed. It must be defined through prayerful and careful conversation. Talk together about what kind of rhythm would best serve your marriage in this season. Talk can only be wise when it happens, so don't allow the delicacy of this topic to go unaddressed. Invite each other to honestly comment on your frequency dial. Is it set at the right level? Why or why not? Don't accuse. Ask questions and listen to your spouse's response. Remember, sex is a conversation topic God has already initiated with us in his Word. Move in with confidence then, believing that God wants to bless your attempts to understand and love each other in better ways.

## The Wise Soul Knows . . . Lasting Intimacy Requires Enduring Grace

> According to the grace of God given to me, like a skilled master builder I laid a foundation, and someone else is building upon it. Let each one take care how he builds upon it. (1 Cor. 3:10)

God gave Paul a great gift—a Spirit-infused ability and power—to build doctrine into Christians, to build up Christians for churches, and to build up churches for the mission of God. God has also given married believers a great gift—a great grace. It's the Spirit-endowed ability and power to build a grace-saturated marriage marked by lasting intimacy. Grace comes built into the marriage covenant. The moment a couple whispers "I do," God begins working hard for the success of their marriage. That success includes grace for spouses to grow more intimate as they age.

A good marriage doesn't need sex to be central. A good marriage doesn't need a sex life loaded with expectations. A good marriage—and good sex, for that matter—needs great grace. Grace not only saves us; it hangs around for the honeymoon and the years to follow (Titus 2:11–15). Grace also has a voice. For spouses seeking to enjoy each other sexually long into the future, grace has some specific things worth hearing.

> A good marriage— and good sex, for that matter— needs great grace.

*First, grace says that "My vision of handsome or beautiful is my spouse"* (Song of Sol. 1:15–16; 4:7). One thing that impresses me about the often-overlooked Old Testament book Song of Solomon is how laser-focused Solomon and his bride are upon one another. Faces and forms are offered with descriptions so vivid one might wonder what the Motion Picture Association rating would be. It reminds me of a popular song from when I was a kid: "I Only Have Eyes for You." When our eyes are rightly fixed on our spouse, cultural definitions of beauty become almost irrelevant. Beauty, as the saying goes, is in the eye of the beholder.

Grace makes our spouse blindingly beautiful to us, and grace keeps them that way for the rest of our lives. Whether they look great in a bathing suit or great in a wheelchair, grace beautifies our spouse for us. It helps us grow more deeply in love even as age exacts its revenge on our appearance. How else can one explain the phenomenon of some beautiful women marrying men who have faces only a mother could love? Grace unlocks the "How did he get her?" astonishment that has existed since the days of the dinosaurs. Grace beautifies what it beholds.

> Grace helps us grow more deeply in love even as age exacts its revenge on our appearance.

*Next, grace says that "The past should stay there."* For newlyweds, the wedding reception is a distraction from the post-ceremony mission—to get alone, get naked, and start the party as soon as possible. A wedding delivers many delights, but few are as sweet as the divine and communal permission to have sex and lots of it (or at least try to). And why not? Enjoying each other sexually is beautiful and natural, a sacred wedding gift from our heavenly Father. The newlywed years become an adventure of exploring each other's bodies and enjoying the intoxication that comes with unwrapping the gift of sex (Prov. 5:18–19).

Yes, abuse, past partners, shame, misinformation, and wrong expectations often make coupling far more complicated than the entertainment industry would have us believe. But most couples see the marriage as a fresh start and want their marriage bed to be a safe, undefiled space where intimacy flourishes (Heb. 13:4). Having said that, even newlyweds can miss the impact of a hazardous intimacy intruder.

Couples often arrive at the altar with what we might call the "X-factor." By this I mean the knowledge of ex-boyfriends, ex-girlfriends, ex-spouses, the reality of past sex partners, or maybe deep regrets about foolish behavior with one another. Regardless of the purity or promiscuity of their path to marriage, every spouse arrives at this magical moment believing that what they'll share together physically will be hallowed and unique. And here's the head game. When newlyweds arrive having already opened the gift of sex, as many do, it can spark unexpected fears about comparisons with past partners, stabs of irrational jealousy, and anxiety or unsettled feelings about whether married sex can be enjoyed.

Dan adored Katy. He told anyone who would listen that meeting her was an undeserved gift sent straight from heaven. Katy had fallen in love with Dan at work, the very moment she saw him help an elderly woman through the door and into her car. They dated for eight months, then set a wedding date.

One evening while they were baring souls and swapping stories, Dan discovered Katy was not a virgin—not even close. Dan wasn't altogether surprised given some of the ways Katy had described her past. He also knew that, if truth be told, he was in no position to judge. It was rumored in certain circles that Dan's college conquests were the stuff of legend. But Dan felt unsettled by the news. Granted, he realized what a chauvinistic hypocrite he was to even give these thoughts mental airtime. Nevertheless, some formless intruder was whispering questions in Dan's ear: *Would their lovemaking be invaded by thoughts from her past? Would he be unconsciously compared or measured against one of Katy's ex-boyfriends? And why did the idea of another man touching his wife just make him feel all kinds of crazy?*

Katy had a tighter grip on the steering wheel. For her, Dan's past was a non-issue. It was ancient history, stuff she could barely remember.

Couples can get stuck on the past in premarital dialogues, during the newlywed nestling, and even during those post-newlywed aftershocks that can arise as two people sort through spending the rest of their life with a sinner. At each stage the struggle with the past is real. But the good news is that it need not be permanent. Good counseling—the kind that guides engaged and married couples into necessary conversations—helps to silence the past and ban it from future visits.

But should it linger, there is something more powerful than good counseling available for couples, pre- or post-wedding. It's grace—unrelenting, stubborn, amazing grace—that gives us the power to forget whispering intruders and fixate on God-honoring matters: "Finally, brothers, whatever is true, whatever is honorable, whatever is just, whatever is pure, whatever is lovely, whatever is commendable, if there is any excellence, if there is anything worthy of praise, think about these things" (Phil. 4:8). The good news is that God's grace ultimately overwrites our separate stories by creating a united future. A sexual life grows richer because we are "forgetting what lies behind and straining forward to what lies ahead" (Phil. 3:13).

Talk to any married couples who have cleared this hurdle and they will quickly confirm that the experience of God uniting them for the future was far more powerful than any memories or entanglements from the past. Take heart. The same will be true for you.

*Third, grace says that "I will not define you by your worst moments."* A lot of sex in marriage either slows or stops because of a certain type of inner narrative. We begin to see the other through their weaknesses, mistakes, or even sins. We label our spouse by their worst moments.

Grace speaks here too. Grace says, "I see beyond your mistakes to the good you intended." Grace refuses to settle on a spousal profile compiled from their weaknesses. When grace looks in the mirror, it says, "By the grace of God I am what I am" (1 Cor. 15:10). When grace looks at our spouse, it says, "It is right for me to feel this way about you, because I hold you in my heart, for you are a fellow partaker with me of grace" (adapted from Phil. 1:7).

Have you ever read Hebrews 11? It's the surprising gallery of faithful Old Testament folks who appear to be randomly dropped into the letter. Tucked within the chapter are names like Samson and Rahab. Some are leaders who rose to great heights before tumbling into deep, dark places. Yet there they are, appearing in Hebrews 11 like Old Testament has-beens undergoing image repair.

What strikes me most deeply about this list is how the author of Hebrews remembers only the best moments of their stories. For Samson and Rahab, it's as if they were plucked out of the trash heap of history and buffed clean by the memories of what they did right.

What amazing grace! So potent that it remembers messed-up people like Samson or Rahab for their best moments. Grace reclaims the past by remembering a person's highlights reel, not simply their outtakes. This is the practical way we live out the truth of the gospel. If Jesus's death and resurrection tell us anything, it's that the worst behavior in our spouse is not the final statement about their life. In the gospel, Christ's life shines through our death. And as our marriage moves forward, we have the opportunity to look at our spouse through the lens of that transforming grace—the very same lens through which God views us. In the light of grace, memories can be redeemed. In the light of grace, we can let what God has done in our spouse define them rather than their failures, and we can let that grace focus our present conversation and future hopes.

## WISE TALK

Look over the previous pages and see the words that grace says to us. Which one seems most relevant to your marriage? Ask your spouse to answer the same question, and listen carefully to their response. Grace acts upon the soul like boiling water. It throws a flame beneath the surface so that impurities can rise to the top of our consciousness. Grace leads us to find the law at work within us (Rom. 7:21) and trains us "to renounce ungodliness and worldly passions, and to live self-controlled, upright, and godly lives in the present age" (Titus 2:12). Are you hearing the voice of grace more clearly? One of you may see things more clearly at first. How

> you respond to that reality, with pride or humility, may determine whether you experience more grace. "But he gives more grace. Therefore it says, 'God opposes the proud but gives grace to the humble'" (James 4:6). Humble yourself before your spouse today. Enjoy more grace. It will tutor you toward wisdom in marriage.

## The Wise Soul Knows . . . Keep a Sense of Humor

Maybe the most practical way to show grace to our spouse is by laughing.

In fact, I think that one must have a touch of madness to enjoy a lasting marriage. Sometimes that means tolerating the same madness, or what may seem to be even more madness, in your spouse. Think about it . . .

Marriage unites two people with remarkably textured stories, and it unites two people who suffer and sin. Then it requires they share a bathroom, bank accounts, and a bed. As a result of all this sharing, we married folk become experts on our spouse's proclivities, peccadillos, bents, flaws, and temptations. Eventually, you can finish your wife's sentence or relocate your husband to the doghouse with nary a glance. Marriage is like a relational WikiLeaks: it exposes all of our classified information—our laziness, depression, greed, anxiety, and arrogance. Marriage outs us.

> One must have a touch of madness to enjoy a lasting marriage.

The only way to survive that kind of exposure is to have a sense of humor. In other words, we must be insane enough to find some laughter amid the fallenness and foibles—both our own and our spouse's. That's the only way to survive the absurdities of the marriage institution. G. K. Chesterton said it well:

> A man and a woman cannot live together without having against each other a kind of everlasting joke. Each has discovered that the

other is a fool, but a great fool. This largeness, this grossness and gorgeousness of folly, is the thing which we all find about those with whom we are in intimate contact; and it is the one enduring basis of affection, and even of respect.[2]

One of the things that makes affection durable, according to Chesterton, is having a long-suffering sense of humor. Weaknesses and eccentricities are no longer irritants but comic relief. So the best thing we can do is learn to laugh at our spouse's foibles . . . and at our own.

One of the best places for a husband and wife to see and retell this "everlasting joke" is when their naked bodies are offered to serve each other. It is glorious when a husband and wife find that their initial years of sexual novelty have matured into seasons of sacred unity and intimacy. Learning over time to serve one another with their bodies is a gift from God they alone possess (1 Cor. 7:3–4). Yes, it takes time, patience, and conversation. But eventually the husband and wife learn to relax together, to give themselves freely, and to seek one another's pleasure instead of the stolen or selfish pleasures that may have characterized their lives before marriage (Prov. 9:17–18).

It's remarkable, mysterious, and glorious that great fools fit together. The two really do "become one flesh" (Gen. 2:24). And more anniversaries bring more laughs.

When kids appear, they arrive with a built-in superpower: sucking the sexual life out of your body and home. As jobs become demanding, a couple's customary sexual rhythm can be affected. Then, over time, our bodies become unruly. They hold water, weight, and gas, and they refuse to part with any of these treasures except the third. Before you know it, gravity takes over and our frames shift south. For men, the hair on our bodies does magic

2. "Chesterton on Dickens," in *The Collected Work of G. K. Chesterton*, vol. 15 (San Francisco: Ignatius, 1989), 188. Quoted in Andy Crouch, *The Tech-Wise Family* (Grand Rapids: Baker Books, 2017), 54.

tricks, disappearing from our heads and reappearing in less attractive places like ears and noses. This broad range of issues makes attempting sex more complicated. It can leave maturing couples with a sex life that resembles a solar eclipse—there are still times when your bodies physically and emotionally align, but sadly the event lasts only five minutes! With all these circumstances stacked against fulfillment in the marriage bed, you've got to learn to laugh. If you don't, you'll end up crying.

It had been a great date night. With four kids at home, the idea of ending the night by going, umm, "parking" was a stroke of genius. Marriages need this kind of zesty spice, I reasoned to Kimm. Let's kill the engine, crank the classic rock, and create the memory. Our zesty spice must have been contagious, because the guy banging on the window had some too. Unfortunately, his spice was confined to his language. Apparently, we'd killed the engine on his property, a gesture he took as an assault on his constitutional rights. He created a memory all right.

> We are all glorious fools who need grace to stay together in a fallen world. Few things deliver it more than laughing together at our folly.

Ten minutes later the police arrived. I tried my best to explain, but those minutes listening to the wild-eyed, commie-busting property owner dictating to me the state and local laws had convinced me I was headed to the slammer. I saw myself, as clear as day, cornered in the prison yard, explaining to tat-covered cons how I got three to five years for parking with my wife. They would perceive the irony and laugh merrily with me. Then they would beat me up.

Fortunately, the police had a better sense of humor than the property owner. We were given a warning and told not to come back. I took that to mean parking was legal, just not there.

We found better places.

Laugh at yourselves. Laugh at your struggles. Laugh at the changes time inflicts. We are all glorious fools who need grace to stay together in a fallen world. Few things deliver it more than laughing together at our folly.

## WISE TALK

I'm a pretty serious personality, so Kimm ends up laughing more than I do. I can struggle sometimes with being in the moment. Sometimes I can take myself too seriously. It's one of the things I most dislike about myself. Kimm, on the other hand, loves this about me. It gives her endless material to laugh about.

Can you relate to my weaknesses? How would your spouse rate your sense of humor? What is it about humor that conveys grace? Talk to each other about the stressors impacting your sexual desires right now. If your desires have been changing lately, talk about why and invite your spouse to think and pray about it with you. When life gets busy, these kinds of conversations can get overlooked. If necessary, schedule a time. Oh, and bring a joke.

### The End of Sex

Sex is super, but it's also temporal. Even when we speak of "lasting sex," we are talking only of this life. There is no marriage in heaven (Matt. 22:30), so it's pretty logical that we won't be having sex. But sex, like marriage, was never meant to be an end in itself. God would never dispose of something so glorious if there weren't something better with which to replace it. Sex was created as a foretaste of something greater—the superior joy and delight we will experience being with Jesus in the new heaven and new earth.

This truth—that marriage is temporary and meant as a "glory sign" to point us to Jesus—may hit you in a couple of different ways. Some of you may be saying, "Good. Sex was always filled with baggage for us and doing without it represents no great loss." Other couples may be deeply disappointed. You'll miss experiencing one another in such an intimate and enjoyable way. You might even ask, "How can God be glorified in heaven by denying us one of the few ecstasies we've experienced on earth?" I love the way C. S. Lewis answered this concern. Here's what he wrote in his book on miracles:

> I think our present outlook might be like that of a small boy, who, on being told that the sexual act was the highest bodily pleasure should immediately ask whether you ate chocolates at the same time. On receiving the answer "No," he might regard absence of chocolates as the chief characteristic of sexuality. In vain would you tell him that the reason why lovers in their carnal raptures don't bother about chocolates is that they have something better to think of. The boy knows chocolate: he does not know the positive thing that excludes it.
>
> We are in the same position. We know the sexual life; we do not know, except in glimpses, the other things which, in Heaven, will leave no room for it.[3]

My friends, the end of sex will be the beginning of something more glorious, something that exceeds the once-a-day demand of a seventy-year-old Starbucks drinker, something better than you can possibly imagine. Pleasure in a sin-saturated world is always muted by our fallenness. But a day is coming when we will slip the bonds of brokenness to experience pleasure in a wholly pure and unobstructed way. An orgasm on earth won't begin to compare to the delight of being in the presence of the divine dance between the persons of the Trinity. There is greater joy in joining in eternal communion with God. That's the end for which we have been created.

So enjoy sex while you have it. But do so remembering that the best is yet to come!

3. C. S. Lewis, *Miracles* (New York: Collier Books, 1960), 159–60.

# Defining Moment #7:
## When You Discover Sex Changes with Age

There are significant shifts that accompany aging and make sex more delicate and difficult. If one lives long enough, sex may be confined to cherished memories. Encountering these changes—which may include the end of your sex life—is a defining moment.

| | The Moment | Our Response |
|---|---|---|
| **The Decision for Truth** | Will I equate intimacy with achieving orgasm? | Or will my understanding of sexuality include communication, intimacy, and affection, preparing me for the day when sex moves to the side? |
| **The Cost Required** | Will my unrealistic vision of what is "normal" heap guilt and shame on my spouse? | Or will we define "normal" together in a way that suits and serves our particular marriage? |
| **The God-Exalting Opportunity** | Will I grow bitter and angry when our sex life doesn't meet—or no longer meets—my expectations? Will I define my spouse by their worst moments? | Or will our sex life be built on grace and joy so that we have eyes only for each other and are able to laugh together even as we age? |
| **The Way It Grows the Soul** | Will I let regret and anxiety over memories and entanglements in the past rob me from joy with my spouse? | Or will I let God's forgiveness overwrite our separate stories and create a new united future for our marriage? |
| **The Way It Sets Our Destination** | Will I be disappointed that there will be no marriage and sex in heaven? | Or will I live and love for the sake of the greater joy that will come in communion with God? |

# ENDING T♥GETHER

DEFINING MOMENT #8:

# When Dreams Disappoint

The Invisible Gorilla. It's an unusual name for a Harvard experiment but an apt description of what happened during this extraordinary survey. The subjects of the experiment were shown a one-minute film of six people passing a basketball. Three players were wearing white shirts and three were wearing dark shirts. The subjects were asked to ignore the dark-shirted people and count the number of passes made by the players in white shirts. When the short video ended, the subjects were asked to report the number of passes they'd counted. The correct answer was fifteen passes.

But the correct answer was immaterial. The test wasn't measuring the subjects' mathematical abilities.

Each subject was thoroughly interviewed to recollect all they observed in the video, and at the conclusion the researcher asked, "Did you see the gorilla?"

In the middle of the experiment, an actor in a gorilla suit strolled into the middle of the basketball tossing, thumped his chest in apelike fashion, and then exited the screen on the opposite side. Of the 60 seconds of filming, the gorilla was present for nine of them. I'm not very good at math, but my calculator tells me that's a full 15 percent.

So, what were the results? *Half the subjects who were shown the video never saw the gorilla.*

My math *is* adequate enough to know that's 50 percent—all so laser-focused on counting passes that they missed a surprising, peculiar development that occurred right under their noses!

And what did the scientists with clipboards prove? Are invisible gorillas really everywhere—from the supermarket to Starbucks—yet undetectable to us?

> What we see is shaped by what we expect to see.

Not exactly. The Invisible Gorilla was a test of perception: would the subjects see something unexpected beyond their obvious task of counting the passes?

The study concluded that what we see is shaped by what we expect to see. Our brains are created in such a way that our vision forms around what we anticipate will happen. Which means that if we are not expecting something—not looking for it to happen—we may completely miss it.

What's true of the gorilla test is true of marriage as well.

## My Dreams for Marriage

Everyone marries with a dream. Our outlook is profoundly shaped by what we expect to see. And many of us entered wedlock so focused on our dreams that we missed some gorilla-like realities.

Dreams do that. We chase them and they intoxicate us, obscuring our vision. The addictive power of a dream makes it difficult to see clearly. And in the field of dreams that makes up life, few exaggerate our expectations more than our dreams of what life will be like in the days after "I do."

Our hopes for matrimony can be as customized as our individual personalities and relationships, but there are some common dreams that, when disappointed, can distress a soul and disorient a marriage. They become defining moments of how—and if—we move forward together.

Let's take a look at three of them.

## Dream #1: Love Will Keep Us Together

If you have ever been to Philadelphia, you may have strolled through Love Park, home of the iconic pop art image sculpted with the letters L-O-V-E. Since the mid-70s, people have stood before this statue and pondered the meaning of its design and message. Is it a religious statement? A political protest? A personal dispatch? An erotic image? I don't know. But I do know this sculpture reflects the way many people think about love. We see it as an exquisite, artful word into which we can pour our own meaning.

> Whether or not love keeps us together depends largely on how we define love.

There's no doubt: love is powerful. When couples enter into marriage, they dream about how love will keep them together through the years. And it can. But whether or not love keeps us together depends largely on how we define love.

"An intense feeling of deep affection" tops the list of dictionary definitions for love,[1] and that's not surprising. Couples believe that feelings—specifically romantic feelings—are expected to endure unabated till death do us part. Romantic comedies, or "rom-coms" in the dialect of Hollywood, support and popularize this notion of dalliances and delights. Rom-coms often end predictably: with a "happily ever after" wedding. The loud message is that here, in marriage, romance finds its forever home.

Now, certainly I'm not going to make a case for the purposes of this illustration that two people who get hitched have to be

---

1. *New Oxford American Dictionary, Third Ed.*, s.v. "love," ed. Angus Stevenson and Christine A. Lindberg (Oxford: Oxford University Press, 2010), Apple OS X electronic edition.

mutually unattractive and emotionally monotonous. I'm simply pointing out that when it comes to marriage, most of us start at a disadvantage. The starting point that our culture has fixed seems decisively centered in appearance, attraction, and emotional attachment. And this vision has shaped our understanding of love as well as our dreams and expectations for what marriage should deliver.

Romance will always be important to marriage. But with kids, careers, and age, it can shift from something we instinctively feel to something for which we must intentionally fight. In a maturing marriage, romance will morph. But while feelings are fickle, there is a kind of love that glues a marriage in a way that creates an enduring bond. The fading of romance and the reality of brokenness becomes a defining moment in marriage.

### Love as Loss

First, love is what we lose. When you love someone, you're losing. I'm not talking about losing a competition. Rather, I'm talking about the kind of love that seals the escape hatch so we lose our freedom to withdraw or retaliate when things get tough.

In 1519, Captain Hernán Cortés arrived by sea on the eastern shores of what is the modern-day Veracruz region of Mexico. On arrival, Cortés issued an order that stunned his men: "Burn the ships!" That's an unusual form of motivation, to be sure. Yet one thing was clear: they lost their way of escape. There was no going back.

> Because commitment and faithfulness lie at the heart of love, marriage means we lose all exits and backup plans.

Love burns the ships. Because commitment and faithfulness lie at the heart of love, marriage means we lose all exits and backup plans. Love toward your spouse is not rooted in how you feel treated. Love doesn't start with fairness or justice, or with who occupies the moral high ground. Love is anchored in the vows we exchange, the promises we make, and ultimately the reality of who Jesus is to us. "We love because he first loved us" (1 John 4:19).

Think about it. Loss, by death on the cross, was the way God displayed to us his heart of love (John 15:13). And loss, by daily death to self, displays our love for one another (Luke 9:23). Elisabeth Elliot said it this way:

> Marriage is death to privacy, independence, childhood's home and family, death to unilateral decisions and the notion that there is only one way of doing things, death to the self. When these little deaths are gladly and wholeheartedly accepted, new life—the glory of sacrificial love which leads to perfect union—is inevitable.[2]

I can hardly count the number of times I've sat with men who assume that marriage shouldn't claim their priorities. I'm not talking about newlyweds here. Back in the day, these men married unprepared to lose themselves in the name of finding a life that engenders a woman's respect, trust, loyalty, sacrifice, and sexuality. They never came to understand that a good marriage is hard to achieve because it requires sacrifice.

I can certainly see myself in this self-centered thinking. Losing myself is hard. I can be inconsiderate because I don't want to lose my freedom. It's natural to think about myself first. I love my own way of doing things. My heart is a like a stallion that refuses to lose, that refuses to be broken. My preferences too quickly determine what we do before I hear Kimm's heart or defer to her desires. Sometimes my selfishness has been so pronounced that I've needed friends to correct me. And that's what maturing love does.

It's really hard, this love thing. Maybe you can relate. Love curbs preferences, prerogatives, and privileges. It eliminates that

2. Elisabeth Elliot, *The Path of Loneliness: Finding Your Way through the Wilderness to God*, reprint ed. (Grand Rapids: Revell, 2007), 71.

walled-off existence that refuses the surrender of vulnerability. "Love demands vulnerability," C. S. Lewis observed:

> Apart from such vulnerability, our hearts grow hard and stiff. Love anything, and your heart will certainly be wrung and possibly be broken. If you want to make sure of keeping it intact, you must give your heart to no one, not even to an animal. Wrap it up carefully round with hobbies and little luxuries; avoid all entanglements; lock it up safe in the casket or coffin of your selfishness. But in that casket—safe, dark, motionless, airless—it will change. It will not be broken; it will become unbreakable, impenetrable, irredeemable.[3]

The world tells us to find ourselves, that to taste the secret sauce of happiness we must love ourselves. Jesus has a different take: "For whoever would save his life will lose it, but whoever loses his life for my sake will save it" (Luke 9:24). Love for God means we abandon one way of living (Gal. 5:16–21) to gain a greater reward (Matt. 6:33; Luke 6:35). To save our soul we must lose our life.

### Love as Gain

This leads us to the other side of the equation. Though love means losing, there is gain as well. Wonderful, glorious, stupendous, surprising delights and blessings await those who commit to one another in marriage. God gives us marriage for our joy. Even as I describe how we must lose ourselves in marriage, I'm not envisioning a form of asceticism. In marriage we embrace loss because of what we gain. And what do we gain? Consider these examples:

- *We gain a promise-centered commitment.* Rashid and Sophie have been married for twenty-eight years. There

---

3. Quoted in Joe Rigney, *Lewis on the Christian Life: Becoming Truly Human in the Presence of God* (Wheaton: Crossway, 2018), 232.

were tough years for sure; times where busyness, an unruly child, depression, and poor communication muted the feelings of love. But the question of their fundamental commitment was never on the table. The afternoon they said "I do," Rashid and Sophie made vows—a set of declarations in one moment that promised future love. They recited their vows before family, friends, and the rector who married them. When the hard times arrived, when feelings of love became less accessible, they stood on the foundation of those promises they'd exchanged. Years later, they're still together, enjoying the sweet fruit of commitments kept. Years of faithful, enduring love have created the kind of companionship and mutual gratitude they never dreamed possible.

- *We gain in godliness.* As a single man, Vijay thought he was spiritually mature. With all-night prayer vigils, multiple Bible studies, and service projects every weekend, certainly the angels in heaven were applauding him as a fine specimen of Christianity. But then Vijay got married. Living with his wife surfaced garbage in his heart he never imagined was there. Vijay loved control, but he married a free spirit. He loved order, and she wasn't very organized. Vijay spent three years trying to change her, only to realize his strong exhortations weren't very loving. After seeking pastoral counsel, Vijay began to see he was attempting to remake his wife in his own image. He repented of his arrogance and received grace to make some important changes. Life became more about loving and serving his wife as better than himself. His capacity for kindness and compassion grew as he sought to understand her thinking and serve her in areas where she was weaker. Vijay also grew sharper in discerning his own temptations and weaknesses as his wife's perspective took on a proportional role in the marriage. By loving his wife better, he grew in godliness.

- *We gain by being known.* Though Lulu had been sober
  for seven years, her past haunted and taunted her with
  a venomous lie: *With what you've done, no one will
  love you.* When she met Ken, Lulu shared some of her
  story—mostly bits and pieces—as a gauge to measure
  his response. Ken was unfazed. He understood that
  everyone has a story of brokenness from which God has
  saved them. Even after their wedding, Lulu would occasionally share other categories from her past, fearing
  each would be the last straw. Ken took it all in stride. In
  fact, there were times he actually cried when he heard
  about her sin and suffering. Eleven years into their marriage, Lulu realized something. Ken *knew* her, warts and
  all, and he loved her anyway! This began to open new
  doors of understanding God's love—an eternal, enduring love that pursued us even while we were still his enemies (Rom. 5:10). Lulu was fully known *and* completely
  accepted by her husband, despite the shame she felt. Her
  husband understood the gospel. He lived aware of all he
  had been forgiven, and he was determined to pass along
  to his bride the astonishing mercy he'd received (Luke
  6:35–38).
- *We gain in endurance.* It was in their seventeenth year of
  marriage that the phone rang. Alex had nervously anticipated this moment. "It's cancer," said the doctor, "the
  bad kind." Cindy grabbed his hand, squeezing hard as the
  color drained from her face. "Treatment will need to start
  immediately." So it began. Cindy was heroic in the way she
  served her suffering husband, and Alex refused to retreat
  into stoic silence. They shared their fears, prayed constantly, cried, and suffered the treatments together. Two
  years later, Alex was pronounced cancer-free. They took a
  vacation to mark the moment. Enduring this trial together
  had drawn them even closer.

And there's more gain, so *much* more! Companionship, trusted friendship, sexual enjoyment—these are just some of the gains that often accompany devoted love. And they illustrate a deep truth, buried like a twinkling diamond in the heart of gospel sacrifice: "For whoever would save his life will lose it, but whoever loses his life for my sake will find it" (Matt. 16:25).

## Dream #2: We'll Always Be Friends

I just mentioned companionship as one of the things we gain in marriage. How can this also be a disappointed dream?

Here's how. There are conditions that must be met in order to build a marriage on the friendship that began in dating. If we ignore these conditions, we're like an iron that's been set up but never used; we easily grow hot, but our issues . . . well, they're never ironed out.

### Lasting Friendship

What are the conditions that must be met for marital friendship to endure?

*First, Jesus must be our friend.* Jesus himself said, "No longer do I call you servants, for the servant does not know what his master is doing; but I have called you friends" (John 15:15). Jesus calls us his friends because we know what the master is doing. God, the Master, is calling us into loving communion with him. He wants us to enjoy intimacy with him and friendship with Jesus. "Fellowship with God," says J. I. Packer, "is the source from which fellowship among Christians springs; and fellowship with God is the end to which Christian fellowship is a means."[4]

Some readers may see this point about friendship and fellowship with God as incidental—like I'm obliged to include something spiritual so we can get to what really matters in the friendship between husband and wife.

---

4. J. I. Packer, *God's Words: Key Bible Themes You Need to Know* (Downers Grove, IL: InterVarsity, 1981), 193.

Not so. Part of the reason the dream of enduring friendship detonates is because the desires for friendship are first horizontal, not vertical. As C. S. Lewis wrote, "Friendship, then, like the other natural loves, is unable to save itself. . . . [It must] invoke the divine protection if it hopes to remain sweet."[5]

Marriage is hard; there are finances, in-laws, sexual adjustments, the arrival of kids (or the fact that kids don't arrive), sickness, lost jobs, teenage angst, conflict, aging, and our sinful responses. How can a person possibly navigate such treacherous terrain? Proverbs answers the question: "There is a friend who sticks closer than a brother" (Prov. 18:24). The ultimate friend who sticks is, of course, Jesus.

*Second, your marital friendship must be your priority.* Never in history has the word "friend" been more dumbed down than in our social media age. First co-opted by Facebook, friendship is now reduced to our list of contacts and virtual acquaintances—they are faces as involved in our lives as strangers we pass on the freeway.

I can remember walking down a set of steps at church one day and observing a circle of young people who'd all grown up together. But rather than exchanging updates on life and love, or even laughing over shared memories or personal oddities, they were all glued to their phones. It was the strangest thing—friends circled up as they'd been for years, except now they weren't communicating with words at all. Their bodies were present but their communication was virtual. "Besties" in a brave new world.

Companionship—the kind that develops into oneness—is one of God's major goals for marriage. At the first wedding in history, cleaving and becoming one flesh were identified as the core benefits of matrimony (Gen. 2:24). These benefits become a reality the moment you say "I do." The challenge comes when couples assume these blessings are installed as mature oaks rather than as tender

5. C. S. Lewis, *The Four Loves* (New York: Harcourt, Brace and Company, 1960), 124.

saplings that must be tended and cultivated. One of the casualties of this idea is that friendships never develop from the pre-wedded romantic stage. As Carolyn G. Heilbrun once said, "Marriage has owed too much to romance, too little to friendship."[6] I agree. This is why developing friendship makes the list of defining moments. Friendship becomes a dream deferred if we don't fight to protect it. "Hope deferred makes the heart sick, but a desire fulfilled is a tree of life" (Prov. 13:12). Prioritizing friendship means our spouse is our first earthly priority. And yes, this means the antiquated face-to-face variety where sitting, looking, sharing, and experiencing each other is not replaced by functional modes of communication. Prioritizing friendship with our spouse also means they aren't becoming slowly displaced by other people with whom we share hobbies or work interests, or who we just enjoy being around. It's great for husbands and wives to have such people in their life. They add spice, interest, and opportunities to serve. But we must proceed carefully, remembering that "A man of many companions may come to ruin" (Prov. 18:24). Ruin follows marriages that don't prioritize the right friendships.

*Third, make room for loneliness.* One of the biggest surprises for married people is that loneliness—the experience that often plagued them as singles—does not get left at the wedding altar. Triggers can include a number of life experiences. Maybe a spouse takes a new job with long, demanding hours. Perhaps an infirm parent moves into the home, requiring constant care. Or maybe parenting teens is just too exhausting. Each of these examples shows how the dream of forever friendship can take a hit.

> Ruin follows marriages that don't prioritize the right friendships.

And loneliness only multiplies if the marital relationship is somehow damaged. Long-standing conflict creates alienation between

6. Quoted in Julia B. Boken, *Carolyn G. Heilbrun*, United States Authors Series (Woodbridge, CT: Twayne Publishers, 1996), 121.

husband and wife. And a divorce or the death of a spouse can cause indescribable disorientation in which a person feels lost, displaced, or even defrauded by God.

Loneliness isn't a single thing or a married thing; it's a Christian thing. We have been called to follow a Savior who was left alone by his closest companions on the night before his death. Even on the cross, Christ hung justifiably forsaken as he bore our sins: "My God, my God, why have you forsaken me?" (Mark 15:34). If we follow Jesus, God will at times call us to bear a similar burden. Even in the happiest marriage, the cross of loneliness cannot be avoided: "If anyone would come after me, let him deny himself and take up his cross daily and follow me" (Luke 9:23).

> In the times when we're exiled, on the outside, misunderstood, and disenfranchised—in these barren wastelands of relationships, God accomplishes some of his deepest work.

Moses experienced loneliness. Many of the prophets did too. David suffered it. Paul as well. We don't fully understand it, but sometimes God draws us into the desert to teach us lessons that can only be learned there. In the times when we're exiled, on the outside, misunderstood, and disenfranchised—in these barren wastelands of relationships, God accomplishes some of his deepest work.

If you're there right now, don't immediately charge your spouse with the crime of making you feel lonely. Loneliness doesn't mean your marriage is in trouble. It means God loves you and is excavating places in your soul. If you feel that's you right now, flee to him. Pour out your heart to his ears of love: "Turn to me and be gracious to me, for I am lonely and afflicted" (Ps. 25:16).

### Steps to Take

Maybe you're reading this section and realizing that while your marriage functions well as a business, it could legitimately file for bankruptcy. What should you do?

- *First, be encouraged.* The clarity you possess at this moment indicates the Spirit of God is working within you in a powerful way: "For the grace of God has appeared, bringing salvation for all people, training us to renounce ungodliness and worldly passions, and to live self-controlled, upright, and godly lives in the present age" (Titus 2:11–12). The Lord is surfacing what truly drives your heart so he can move you toward actions that will cultivate greater friendship.

> Loneliness doesn't mean your marriage is in trouble. It means God loves you and is excavating places in your soul.

- *Next, it's important for you to tell your spouse what you see.* The conversation doesn't need to be wrapped in a tight package where you have repented sufficiently and are already seeing fruit. Sometimes pride and control cravings make us want to appear spiritual and mature even in our confessions. Just tell your spouse what God is doing in your heart. Acknowledge any areas where you believe you have failed, and talk about the areas where you desire to grow. Then pray.

- *Last, cultivate a deeper friendship.* But beware—you may not feel like doing this. Though it may seem your discussion is sufficient, you must add action to your confession. This may feel like a dead work at first. But the more you seek to open up, ask good questions, enjoy some experiences together, surprise them with a phone call, encourage them with something specific, plan an overnight getaway, insist they spend time with other friends and help make it happen, the more you will rekindle your most precious friendship. Remember, when it comes to rekindling the fire of friendship, actions precede feelings. Act now.

## Dream #3: We Can Live with No Regrets

Stay married for more than a couple of decades and you will have regrets. We're not omniscient, omnicompetent beings who always achieve what we want. We let things slip. We battle weariness. We prioritize wrongly. We miss important family times for things that are, well, less important.

Have you ever made a bad financial decision? Kimm and I recently moved all of our earthly possessions into a storage unit. We haven't become minimalists; we just made a poor decision on a house purchase and it's made life very complicated. From the length of the sale (twenty months), to the moving of our stuff, to the closing of the sale . . . well, let's just say it was an experience I don't want to repeat. Our stuff now sits in a storage unit that cooks under the Florida sun. That house was an unhelpful choice for our marriage and our future. I regret it.

As long as you draw breath you will have regrets.

A man once told me about a family event he was planning called "No Regrets." To me the name suggested that the event was organized by a naïvely wide-eyed newlywed. The couple with no regrets, after all, needs to think a little deeper. If no categories emerge from that exercise, just ask your kids. Regrets orbit around married couples like paparazzi circling the British royal family.

> Regrets orbit around married couples like paparazzi circling the British royal family.

But the gospel meets us in the flood of that flaw-drenched place. Jesus chooses people with regrets as vessels to display his glory. Peter denied Christ three times and fled in the Savior's moment of greatest need. It's difficult to imagine, even after he was forgiven and called (John 21:15–19), that Peter never felt regret. If we're going to make sense of the gospel, we must see ourselves in Peter's failure. People who don't make any mistakes don't need the good news. As Jesus says, "Those who are well have no need of a physician, but those who are sick. I came not to call the righteous, but sinners" (Mark 2:17).

So we must own our regrets. But it's also necessary to see that Christ offers us something far better than merely escaping regret. Through the cross, he reminds us that our stumbles are never big enough to interrupt his plan for our lives. For Peter, and for all of us, there is hope beyond regret. Because our glorious Substitute died and rose again, "No regrets" is scribbled over with "No record."

> We can live and lead with hope even amid broken dreams— not because we will get it all right but because we follow a Savior who did.

Do you see how this changes the way we think about our marriage? We can live and lead with hope even amid broken dreams— not because we will get it all right but because we follow a Savior who did. Only from that cradle of security can we admit selfishness, loneliness, and regrets. And from that humble posture we can lift our eyes to the One who promises to take even what we perceive as losses and griefs and make them into something beautiful. As the psalmist says:

> You have turned for me my mourning into dancing;
>   you have loosed my sackcloth
>   and clothed me with gladness,
> that my glory may sing your praise and not be silent.
>   O LORD my God, I will give thanks to you forever!
>   (Ps. 30:11–12)

## The Gorilla Lesson

Together we've discovered that people often see marriage not as a means of personal or marital growth but as a right due to them in their quest for personal fulfillment. As a means to becoming happy and whole. But that's the fulfillment of a dream not rooted in reality. Such dreamers refuse to acknowledge a fundamental truth: *we never fully know the person we marry*. And if we know who they are now, we can't know the five to six different people they will become over the next fifty years of life.

The minute you marry, a new civilization begins. As a result of your union, you and your spouse will begin to change in profound ways. We're hopeful about the anticipated trajectory, but it's impossible to know. Uncovering this unexpected reality triggers the defining moment in each marriage. What do we do when we discover things we didn't see? How will we respond when profound changes take place in the person we now feel stuck with? What does our response say about our real dreams for marriage? Only a commitment to faithfully pursue God and each other will lock us down for a lifetime of love and friendship.

Remember the Invisible Gorilla? I thank God for that Harvard study. It reveals that what we see is shaped by what we expect to see. Our dreams of marriage and what it should be are a powerful influence. Exposing a few of those expectations will help you to see the bigger picture of God's plan.

The truth is that our dreams can seem to limit God. But he's at work doing more than we can see.

# Defining Moment #8:
## When Dreams Disappoint

Everyone marries with a dream. Our outlook on marriage is profoundly shaped by what we expect to see. When a dream is disappointed, it can distress a soul and disorient a marriage.

| | The Moment | Our Response |
|---|---|---|
| **The Decision for Truth** | Will I focus only on achieving my dreams for this marriage? | *Or* will I see God at work in unexpected times and places where my dreams are disappointed? |
| **The Cost Required** | Will I refuse to let marriage claim my priorities, freedom, and self-centered thinking? | *Or* will I embrace the kind of love that curbs preferences, prerogatives, and privileges? |
| **The God-Exalting Opportunity** | Will I see the dreams of marriage as rights due to me in my quest for personal fulfillment? | *Or* will I see the moments when dreams disappoint as opportunities for personal and marital growth? |
| **The Way It Grows the Soul** | Will I dream of love only as an intense feeling of romantic affection? | *Or* will promise-centered love that results in godliness, vulnerability, and endurance define our marriage? |
| **The Way It Sets Our Destination** | Having neglected the friendship I have with my spouse, focusing only on what's functional and urgent, will I give up pursuing them and wallow in loneliness or the feeling that I've been led astray or defrauded? | *Or* will I pursue my spouse— opening up, asking good questions, planning shared experiences, and encouraging them with service and surprises— with the goal of rekindling our friendship? |

**DEFINING MOMENT #9:**

# When the Kids Leave

Tammy left home for college.

Joe snagged a job in another city.

Christa enlisted in the military; she's off to boot camp.

Sean drifted off to another state to be with his friends.

Kim enrolled in vocational school . . . four hundred miles away.

Empty rooms. Deserted spaces. Vacant chairs at the table. It all happens so quickly. The frenzy of keeping teens on time ends abruptly, like a braking roller coaster at an amusement park. One minute you're holding on for dear life. The next thing you know, the ride skids to a halt.

Your kids have gone, and you're left with this surreal, disorienting morass of emotions, trying to figure out why everyone disappeared. Who are you when you're no longer needed as a counselor, chauffeur, banker, chef, or sheriff?

Sweet Honey in the Rock, an African American acapella ensemble, adapted a poem by Khalil Gibran titled "On Children." If you've ever watched your kid say "I do" and then kissed them good-bye, the words of this song toll like an old bell within your soul:[1]

> Your children are not your children.
> They are the sons and daughters of Life's longing for
>   itself.
> They come through you but not from you,
> And though they are with you yet they belong not to you.

The song goes on to describe how we give our kids affection, shelter, and direction, but we can't control what they take, "for they have thoughts of their own." We love our kids, but we can't determine their futures.

## When Your Kids Get Married

It's enough to negotiate a child leaving home. But when our kids get married, there are unique dynamics that unveil some deeply embedded dreams. We know cleaving results in leaving (Gen. 2:24), but who knows what leaving really means until you experience it? Maybe it's just leaving the house or the neighborhood. Whatever it means, it certainly can't mean we're too distant to enjoy Sunday afternoon meals together, right?

Cheryl called her daughter each week to see if they wanted to have Sunday lunch. The ninety-minute drive made it easy to visit each other or just meet in the middle. But the constant calls began to feel like Cheryl wanted more than just time with the newlyweds. Cheryl loved her daughter and new son-in-law, but she was grieving the loss of an entire way of life. It was hard to let go.

If your child's marriage doesn't feel like some kind of irrevocable arrangement has transpired, then you've clocked out of reality. Marriage shuffles the relational network, and one of the places

---

1. Sweet Honey in the Rock, "On Children," *Breaths*, track 12 (Flying Fish, 1988), compact disc.

we feel this most is when our kids get married. Welcoming a new son-in-law or daughter-in-law into your family means giving them a front-row seat to your family's delights . . . and dysfunctions. Your son or daughter's new spouse might have values, routines, and rhythms that reflect the same ethos with which you raised your child. But they might not. Welcoming that new son- or daughter-in-law into your family often feels like a cross-cultural experience.

> Welcoming that new son- or daughter-in-law into your family often feels like a cross-cultural experience.

Every family is its own civilization, complete with culture, dialect, and treasured artifacts. A newlywed spouse's first exposure may feel less like a homecoming and more like the early pilgrims discussing Thanksgiving Day plans with their new Native American acquaintances. They feel awkward, like a stranger in a strange land, speaking a foreign language. And when you look at them, you agree. It feels strange because it is strange. Jesus said, "For this reason a man will leave his father and mother and be united to his wife, and the two will become one flesh" (Matt. 19:5 NIV). God designed marriage to create new families. And when your son or daughter starts a new family, it means they've *left* yours.

As young couples, we typically think about this in terms of geography: "I'm moving out of my parents' house and moving in with my new wife across town." But when you marry off one of your kids, you discover their new marriage also alters your authority and responsibility. There's a seismic shift in your role. You don't stop being Mom and Dad, but you can't expect to be honored or followed in the same way you were when the kids were young. How time is spent, the frequency of being together, where holidays happen, your expectations for seeing grandchildren, the way counsel or opinions are shared—all of these glorious blessings must move out of the realm of authority and expectation and into the realm of influence and collaboration.

Letting go of a son or daughter is a significant test. It reveals how much we trust God's sovereignty in our kids' lives; it reveals where our own emotional security is rooted; and it reveals, in a significant way, what we truly understand about leadership.

## Anticipating the Way Authority Changes

When kids are young, we parents have to establish that we are the authority in the family. Toddlers are taught "attentive obedience." You obey *right away* because your parents love and protect you. Children should come when they're called because Mom and Dad know best. We're bigger. We have more life experience. We're more aware of potential danger, so we should be in charge. And the truth is, establishing your authority when your kids are small isn't that difficult. I don't mean to be dismissive about strong-willed children and the terrible twos. But at the end of the day, it's way easier to lead someone who can be influenced by the threat of withholding cereal. Also, you're just bigger and wiser than your little kids, so it's easy to tell them what to do. What are they going to do about it? Even if they scream for hours, eventually they fall asleep.

As our kids grow, however, we naturally begin to lose some of that type of authority. A son may grow taller and stronger than his mom. A daughter may get wise enough to outsmart her dad. Older kids cry less, but they have tactics. They learn to negotiate, to play Mom and Dad against each other, and eventually to take the car keys and leave without asking. Whether we like it or not, we have to allow older kids to make their own choices. Here's the truth: God designed parenting—like all forms of leadership—so that over time we give our kids away.

If we don't embrace this truth, we'll grow demanding and angry. In fact, a parent unwilling to give up their authority over their children reminds me of King Nebuchadnezzar.

In Daniel 2, King Nebuchadnezzar has a nightmare. But this dream, peculiar and haunting in its particulars, has a cryptic echo of truth. Now awake, a troubled Nebuchadnezzar assembles a cohort of counselors to search for the dream's interpretation. Nothing unusual there. If you're a king with a bad dream that seems freakishly real, getting some help represents good government action.

But Nebuchadnezzar has an absurd expectation. The one who helps him, he decrees, must supply not only the interpretation of the dream but the dream itself. In the world of dream divination, this is a whole new set of metrics. "The word from me is firm," Nebuchadnezzar insists. "If you do not make known to me the dream and its interpretation, you shall be torn limb from limb, and your houses shall be laid in ruins" (Dan. 2:5). If one person doesn't step forward with prophetic knowledge, Nebuchadnezzar is going to exterminate his entire cabinet!

Freeze the frame for a second. Why in the world is Nebuchadnezzar so upset? He's about to burst a blood vessel because no one knows the specifics of his bad dream. He wants a dream reader, which is, I guess, a mind reader who works the night shift. What could save his advisers?

> When a person is empowered with authority—whether at work, in the church, or in the home—the heart begins a war with expectation. The more it loses, the larger its demands grow.

Only hours before the slaughter, God uses Daniel to provide what Nebuchadnezzar demands. But his saving grace shouldn't obscure the drive behind this royal decree. When a person is empowered with authority—whether at work, in the church, or in the home—the heart begins a war with expectation. The more it loses, the larger its demands grow.

It works this way. With leadership come certain privileges and prerogatives. That young toddler learns to obey right away. Pretty soon they learn to fetch the remote for you. They're good at it. They even enjoy doing it! There's nothing inherently wrong with that, until Dad learns to *expect* this from his child. At first we appreciate the good job our child is doing. But then we come to feel we *deserve* a certain response, so when we ask the toddler to fetch the remote and they say "No!" there's a sudden temptation to be outraged. Why so angry? It's more than a simple desire to correct the child's preschool rebellion.

Do you see? A seemingly subtle yet altogether radical transformation has occurred. We have swelled with the significance we think we have, so our blessings become our rights. We now think we deserve what our children give to us. And our identity, which should be anchored outside of our parental role and grounded in what Christ accomplished, has adhered to our position as a father or mother. Because we hold the role, we begin to demand certain benefits as well.

In understanding the leadership role of parents over time, it's clear that earthly parents exercise a type of *diminishing authority* in the lives of their children. As a child matures and the relationship evolves, the parents' responsibility for the child changes and the scope of the parents' daily power is reduced. In other words, their authority is not an unalterable gift from God but a *shifting role* that must adapt to the kid's needs and maturity level. This diminishing of parental responsibility is typically symmetrical to the maturity of the child. In fact, parental authority experiences permanent shifts through certain milestones: leaving home, marriage, and the birth of grandchildren. Certainly, we will always retain the privilege and honor of being mothers and fathers (Exod. 20:12), but hands-on authority and responsibility pass with time.

C. S. Lewis foresaw this shifting role:

> But the proper aim of giving is to put the recipient in a state where he no longer needs our gift. We feed children in order that they may soon be able to feed themselves; we teach them in order that they may soon not need our teaching. Thus a heavy task is laid upon this Gift-love. It must work towards its own abdication. We must

aim at making ourselves superfluous. The hour when we can say "They need me no longer" should be our reward.[2]

Where preadolescent forms of responsibility and authority are exercised on adult children, the results are typically disastrous. But wise parents in a healthy family recognize that the child's maturity has altered their role and changed the nature of their relationship. Having said this, I have to be honest that adapting to these changes is a struggle for us all. Even in the healthiest of family structures, two traps tend to snag us parents of adult children.

### Trap #1: The Demanding Parents

It's rare for a young couple to start a new family with mature humility. I didn't, and you probably didn't either. It's especially difficult when we meet our new spouse's family for the first time. We learn about Uncle Ned, whose singular charm is that he remains pantless at family functions. There may even be a history of addiction and strained relationships you didn't anticipate. When a young man or woman discovers the "dear" souls from whom their spouse hails, there can be a temptation to judge . . . or to try to convince your spouse of the superiority of your own family's customs.

> It's rare for a young couple to start a new family with mature humility.

Over time, if we mature, we learn that talking to our spouse about any weakness we experience in their family requires grace and charity. We also learn to enter family interactions with low expectations and a posture of humility. We learn to celebrate the good, discern the bad, and avoid overreaction. After all, the Bible tells us, "Pay to all what is owed to them . . . respect to whom respect is owed, honor to whom honor is owed" (Rom. 13:7); and near the top of God's list for being honored are the mom and dad (Deut. 5:16).

2. C. S. Lewis, *The Four Loves* (New York: Harcourt, Brace and Company, 1960), 76.

But what happens when the tables are turned?

What happens when you're releasing your child to a new spouse? What happens when your son or daughter, whom you've trained to honor your family's traditions for years, suddenly brings an intruder into your home, one who struggles to accept your customs? Are you able to be patient and gentle with this new whippersnapper? Or are you tempted to get angry and demand respect?

Nebuchadnezzar had grown large, and his expectations had inflated into entitlements. His self-importance produced unreasonable demands because he saw himself as worthy of ultimate respect. In King Nebuchadnezzar's life, he wanted better help, even perfect help. A good want ad might have read:

Only those with godlike abilities need apply! The king deserves it. His dreams require it. Pity the poor counselor who has a bad day. Few things peeve a king more than having people around him who don't know his unspoken dreams. Those unable to deliver on the king's unreasonable or unsearchable goals receive his fury.

Maybe you've never had a Nebuchadnezzar-sized temper. We have quieter ways of fuming, like bitterly comparing our family to others we deem inferior. *We have standards*, we think. Or even directly putting down your son- or daughter-in-law's family to make yourself look better.

Where does such passive-aggressive anger come from?

Pay careful attention to what makes you angry, because what incites your wrath reveals your heart. I remember barking at one of my kids because he made a mistake that made me look bad. I mean, kids are born to make their dads look good, right? In this instance, he was failing at one of the very reasons for his existence! The nerve! Expectations become irrational when the soul swells with self.

> Pay careful attention to what makes you angry, because what incites your wrath reveals your heart.

Thankfully, when I returned home, the Spirit of God was waiting for me with the sweet gift of conviction. And guess what? My anger was not righteous, as I so often assume. It was the wounded pride of a father whose reputation was momentarily scratched. Out of the abundance of self-love, my heart spoke (Matt. 12:34).

But the gospel spoke louder. Loud enough for me to hear—to repent and return to my son with a contrite heart.

The gospel is God's pin to pop the puffy hearts and puncture the bloated heads of entitled parents. I'm grateful for his faithful pricks that reduce my pride and restore my heart to its proper proportion. When I can't hear the gospel, I grow large, my expectations swell, and my mind visits some strange places and absurd ideas. Just like Nebuchadnezzar.

### Trap #2: The Needy Parents

You hear the toast all the time: "I'm not losing a son; I'm gaining a daughter!" (or vice versa). It's a nice sentiment that can make a fiancée feel a deeper connection to their new extended family. But sometimes that statement tows the freight of emotional and relational expectations. Before we let our kids go, we need to ask ourselves these questions: Do we see ourselves as a source of emotional love and care *for* the newlyweds, or do we require, either consciously or unconsciously, emotional support *from* the newlyweds? Are we adding burdens, sparing burdens, or lifting burdens?

Lester always had a dream. It started with five kids—two strapping boys and three dainty girls. Having come from a broken home himself, Lester understood the importance of family. He would tell you that family ranked third, after God and church, in his top three priorities. But if you measured the conversation around the house and dinner table, family actually displaced God and church by a ratio of five to one. In Lester's view, families prayed together, stayed together, and stuck together. When the kids grew up and got married, that simply added more seats at the table. It was family expansion, with Lester as a sort of extended family patriarch.

Growing up, Lester never had a stable family, so he needed his own to remain close. He understood "leaving father and mother" to mean his kids would change their residence. But he couldn't imagine them leaving the state.

Ask Lester's kids how they felt and they would've summed it up in one word: *pressure.* They love their dad, but in addition to the normal pressure of accommodating an array of family traditions and juggling other in-laws on holidays, there was the added pressure to never disappoint Dad.

Lester had some things turned around. To be a parent is to bear the emotional burdens of your kids, not to pressure and manipulate them into meeting your felt needs. The healthiest kind of family system is where the parents hold up a mirror for their kids.[3] A parent with a mirror helps their kids put language to their emotions. The child begins to develop vocabulary around the interior life, which helps to solidify the core self. That kind of mirroring of emotions is essential for a child to understand that they are loved, valued, and accepted.

> The healthiest kind of family system is where the parents hold up a mirror for their kids. A parent with a mirror helps their kids put language to their emotions.

In a dysfunctional setup, however, the mirror is swapped. Because the parents' needs take precedence, the kids are left holding the mirror, reflecting back to the parents what the parents want and need to see. When this happens, children learn to play a particular role in the family—the role of stabilizing the parents emotionally.

Lester didn't see his married kids as parts of newly formed families; instead, he saw these new families as extensions of his old one. He felt entitled to his adult kids' time, initiative, and emotional support, particularly during holidays.

3. I'm grateful to Jack Nicholson, founder and president of SageQuest Consulting, for his insight on needy parents and the analogy of the mirror.

Like Mrs. Bennet in *Pride and Prejudice*, needy parents attempt to fulfill their own desires through their kids. This may be rooted in their own family history, in patriarchal expectations, or simply in a misapplication of Scripture that obligates the kids to the parents' wishes. Psychologists call what they are doing "emotional enmeshment." Whatever you call it, it always backfires. Mrs. Bennet's behavior does more harm to her daughters' chances at marriage than it helps. She encourages the bad behavior of Kitty and Lydia and attempts to push Elizabeth into a marriage she doesn't want. She's a literary picture of what it looks like to put burdens on our children rather than lift burdens from them (compare Matt. 23:4 and Matt. 11:28–30).

Kids who grow up in this sort of unhealthy environment can sometimes retain a solid sense of self. But more often they have enmeshed their identity with the approval of their parents. You just can't hold the mirror for parents and have both. Most of the time kids don't have the comprehension or strength to risk the fear of disappointing—or even being abandoned by—their parents, so they accommodate and capitulate to their parents' needs. A child in this sort of family may describe it this way: "If I play my role, Mom and Dad are stable. But if I don't, there will be an emotional price to pay." Kids like these live holding the mirror.

### So . . . What Should I Do?

A child leaving the nest, be it through marriage or some other pursuit, raises instinctive issues in moms and dads. It's good to know and anticipate the temptations that may beset you, but it's also important to know how you'll respond when these issues arrive. How do healthy parents prepare to let their kids go? Here are a few things to consider.

- *Anticipate the emotional impact.* Guilt, grief, regret, nostalgia, anxiety, loss, and aimlessness. These are all common responses for parents navigating the emptying of their nest. Read the book of Psalms and see how the psalmists dealt with similar feelings of loss, anxiety, and change. Let God's Word feed your soul. Spend sufficient time alone. Open your soul to the Lord and allow him to ground your feelings. Remember, it's not your kids' job—just like it's not your spouse's job—to fulfill your dreams or satisfy your longings. Only Christ can satisfy your soul.

- *Anticipate some distance.* It's not personal, and it's not some statement about your parenting. Newlyweds have an entirely new world to become accustomed to. The same is true for a young man or woman working and living alone for the first time. Working things out on their own is important for their training and growth because they'll confront larger issues in the future. If your kids have gotten married, they're learning to walk out the reality of what it means to "leave father and mother and hold fast" to their new spouse (Gen. 2:24). This passage can be painful for us as parents, but it's utterly essential for our married kids.

- *Consider your own marriage.* It's likely your marriage had to adjust around the pace and pressures of the teenage years. Many empty nesters watch their kids say "I do" or "so long" and find they have little to discuss apart from the kids. Recognize this inevitability and prepare now. What books will you want to read together? What hobbies might you enjoy? How might the church be served by your spare time? Have you talked at all about traveling? Learn to see letting go of the kids as an opportunity to rekindle parts of your relationship that were put on the back burner when kids were around.

- *Be the mirror for your kids.* Here are some really important things kids who are on their own need to hear from their parents: "It's not your job to fulfill our dreams. We love to be with you, but we don't need you to be here. We want to empower you to cast your own vision for family visits and the holidays, and you have full permission to let us down." When we speak empowering words like these, our kids will begin to see themselves as valued and their life choices as respected in our eyes.

- *Finally, think about serving.* Adult children often wonder whether their parents are reaching out to satisfy some unmet need or walk back through nostalgia alley. Surprise them by making your phone calls about how you can be of service to them. How can you pray for them? Where are their needs right now? Do they have any projects where they need assistance? Are they ready for a babysitter? Positioning yourself among your kids as one who serves may end up getting you invited to the table more often (Luke 22:27). But whether it does or not, being a servant is what honors God, and it's simply healthier than always needing to be served by your children.

One disclaimer here. I often encourage experienced parents to leave a legacy for the next generation by sharing what they've learned about marriage with their newlywed kids. That's an important service opportunity, but always tread carefully and guard your heart to avoid being self-serving. You might say something like this: "We would be honored to share our thoughts and encouragements with you. They may be of help, but we will always ask permission. And if we do this poorly, please let us know."

## The Ultimate Parent

God shows us what it looks like to be the ultimate parent, always giving support rather than needing it. He shows us how to give away authority and respect rather than clinging to it like Nebuchadnezzar. And for this virtue we need to look to a better king, the One who didn't consider equality with God—and the honor and respect that came with that position—as something to use to his advantage, but who instead emptied himself and took the form of a servant (Phil. 2:5–11).

Empty rooms, deserted spaces, and vacant chairs at the table are a short-lived burden confined to this life. The "I do's" of this life point to the ultimate "I do," when the Bride is finally ready and meets her heavenly Bridegroom for the great wedding feast. When we arrive in the new heaven and new earth, we will be reunited with all believers from whom we've been separated. And we will sit and celebrate without any worries that the time is growing short. We will have all the time we could ever want to share with the ones we love. Eternity will be ours, because time will be no more.

# Defining Moment #9:
## When the Kids Leave

A child leaving the nest, be it through marriage or some other pursuit, raises instinctive issues in moms and dads. It's good to know and anticipate the temptations that may beset us, but it's also important to know how you'll respond when these issues arrive.

| | The Moment | Our Response |
|---|---|---|
| **The Decision for Truth** | Do I require, either consciously or unconsciously, emotional support *from* our adult children? | *Or* do I see myself as a source of emotional love and care *for* our adult children? |
| **The Cost Required** | Do I expect or even feel that I deserve certain responses from our adult children? | *Or* will I understand that our role as parents shifts and that our authority must diminish as the kids grow older and eventually leave home? |
| **The God-Exalting Opportunity** | Will I, like old Nebuchadnezzar, demand that our kids meet all of my expectations? | *Or* will I look to the better king, the One who didn't consider equality with God as something to use to his own advantage, but who instead emptied himself and took the form of a servant (Phil. 2:5–11)? |
| **The Way It Grows the Soul** | Will I need our children to be mirrors for me, expecting them to reflect back what I want and need to see? Will I need them to play the stabilizing role in our life and family? | *Or* will I root my emotional life in my walk with God and be a mirror *for* our kids, helping them to see that they are loved, valued, and accepted? |
| **The Way It Sets Our Destination** | Will I feel betrayed and abandoned by empty rooms, deserted spaces, and vacant chairs? | *Or* will I find my ultimate satisfaction in God alone and learn to see the opportunities he's given me to grow in a new stage of life? |

# CHAPTER 11

DEFINING MOMENT #10:

# When You Learn Closure Is Overrated

Rain pelted the sand as wisps of fog circled the water. Rhoda, the film's eight-year-old protagonist, strutted defiantly, even malevolently, toward the pier. Her vacant eyes concealed a restless evil, the unnamed stimulus behind her unspeakable crimes. Suddenly, a bolt of lightning split the sky and, with almost surgical vengeance, struck the very spot where she stood. Rhoda simply evaporated. The undeniable message was that this bad seed had been tried, found guilty, and sentenced in the courts of heaven. The penalty was death.

To say this movie, *The Bad Seed* (1956), freaked out my eight-year-old brain doesn't begin to describe the trauma. When I say "freaked out," I mean I lost three weeks of sleep poring over my short life for "bad seed" signs within me. I woke up my parents so many times they threatened to make me watch it again if I ever, *ever* came back in their room. They just didn't get it. I mean, sure, there had to be differences between Rhoda and me. But what if God missed these distinctions? Half a century later, I can assure you that there are few devices better designed to tease fear from an undeveloped brain than lying in bed pondering whether your misdeeds will escape the lightning bolt of God's justice. To this day I think the movie was Warner Bros.' way of transforming kids from naughty to nice. It totally worked for me—at least for a few days.

Recently, I read something pretty ironic about the novel on which the cinematic psycho-thriller that scarred me was based. At the end of the book, it's actually the mother who dies—evil Rhoda lives on. But based on the Motion Picture Production Code, a set of moral guidelines for the film industry, the Motion Picture Association of America (MPAA) determined the ending of the movie had to change. The book's conclusion broke one of their cardinal codes for motion pictures at that time: *When evil appears, it must meet justice.* Wickedness can't remain unaddressed or unanswered; it has to be resolved by the end of the movie. So they rewrote the ending and had God torch Rhoda.

It's funny to discover that there was a time when the ratings worked that way. I wish we had that option in real life. Wouldn't it be nice if there was a group authorized to rewrite our endings so that every wrong is resolved, every regret is miraculously redeemed, and every evil is brought to justice? But a broken world has no MPAA rewriting our stories to ensure resolution. There are no contracts to guarantee that closure will happen or that we'll leave life's theater satisfied because everything was tidied up and topped with a nice cherry.

No, in a fallen world there is no guarantee of closure or that happiest of endings.

I hate that. It makes life seem so vulnerable. So unpredictable. And I find that the older I get, the more this absence of closure works like a pebble in my shoe. The longer I walk, the more it aches. But over the years I've discovered something. In the world of marriage, how we relate to those open-ended spaces—the areas where we lack closure—can become defining moments in our life.

What does a married couple do when hard things continue, when the problems seem hopelessly open-ended? How do we make sense of situations where resolution would appear to bring so much glory to God? How do we go on when that experience remains elusive and unreachable, taunting our hopes? How should we respond when a lack of resolution becomes so oppressive and burdensome that a marriage risks collapsing under the strain?

Many of you who are reading this know exactly what I'm talking about.

- Your spouse says horrible things to you and shows no signs of change.
- Despite your efforts at kindness, your in-laws act more like outlaws.
- Birth defects effectively eliminate any hope for a child having a normal life.
- Your spouse commits adultery and leaves for another man or woman. Apart from a miracle, there are no signs of repentance or a return to the life you once enjoyed.
- Your church splits. The community you once enjoyed is now polarized and fragmented.
- You suffer through a shocking divorce in which . . . well, let's just say things got ugly.
- Despite your many appeals and pleas for forgiveness, the Christian friend you sinned against will no longer speak with you.
- Your spouse is suffering and there is no sign of relief.
- After you've prayed for months that your job will improve, your company suddenly downsizes and encourages you to "explore other options."
- Your teenager runs away with no plans of returning. After a few weeks you realize that they are moving on with life.

Your dreams for these years are blown from your hand like ashes in the wind.

- Life with your spouse is, well—*boring*! And there's no sign of change anytime soon.

Deep inside each of us is a desire to make sense of why things happen—particularly those things that have left open, painful wounds. We want to know what it is supposed to mean, which might then supply us with some inside intel on how long something is going to last. We have a sense that we can endure—even for a long time—if we know resolution is coming. But persevering without hope of closure, particularly within the context of marriage, can bewilder us.

After all, this mind-set seems logical. It was in the conversion contract, wasn't it? Or maybe it was just an implied understanding with God. If we love Jesus and try to live by the Bible, then he always has our back. We know he loves us with an everlasting love, so in this arrangement it feels like God owes us a little closure and resolution to these unanticipated difficulties. I mean, he's on our team, right?

> Persevering without hope of closure, particularly within the context of marriage, can bewilder us.

But life is baffling. Marriage in a fallen world brings emotional heartache. We feel a gaping hole in our hearts when we realize that what we signed up for—with both Jesus and our spouse—doesn't deliver all the answers we anticipated. *If God were really present*, we think, *he would resolve the pain and complexity*. As God's child, having a tightly wrapped life should be one of the perks, right? But, dagnabbit, life remains open-ended. And it remains open-ended for periods that push us far beyond our faith, our determination, and our expectations for marriage.

What do we do? Where do we turn when we feel we need certain outcomes in our marriage to move forward? How do we live without becoming cynical—without feeling like marriage, and God, have defrauded us?

The complexity and importance of these questions is why learning to live with a lack of closure becomes our next defining moment in marriage.

## A Fallen World Makes Life Open-Ended

My father had his share of faults, but being late was not among them. His value for timeliness went deep. Speed limits and stop signs became posted suggestions when my old man had an appointment. He'd rather lose a limb than be tardy. When it came to punctuality, my dad was in a league of his own.

But Dad was not perfect. He was subject to the laws and limitations of life in a fallen world—a world where closure, resolution, and absolute consistency are impossible. In this world, even the people we love and who love us most aren't able to always be there. When cancer came calling, my father—the ex-Navy steelworker who'd been married to my mom for thirty-seven years—fought like a heavyweight champ, but he lost.

Even though we enter the new life of God's kingdom at conversion (Col. 1:13), we still inhabit a fallen world. The kingdom is present, but it is not yet consummated. Salvation has come, but brokenness and death persist. Remember the second nested circle from chapter 2? We are fallen beings with decaying bodies. The power of sin has been broken, but its presence remains.

I don't know if you've ever thought about this, but those realities yoke us to inconsistent people and to times in which a lack of closure *will remain*. For instance, the person who builds a marriage on the absolute predictability of their spouse, even a Christian spouse, quickly experiences reality and then perhaps disillusionment. Country singer Billy Currington nailed this irony: "God is great, beer is good . . . and people are crazy!"

I remember once reading 2 Timothy—Paul's final letter, his last will and testament—and being amazed by his unresolved relational landscape: "You are aware that all who are in Asia turned away from me, among whom are Phygelus and Hermogenes" (2 Tim. 1:15). You can almost feel the pain behind these words. You may have had a bad day, but what's it like to have an entire province desert you?

Phygelus and Hermogenes left him, but Paul's just getting started. Now he gets specific:

> But avoid irreverent babble, for it will lead people into more and more ungodliness, and their talk will spread like gangrene. *Among them are Hymenaeus and Philetus, who have swerved from the truth*, saying that the resurrection has already happened. *They are upsetting the faith of some.* (2 Tim. 2:16–18, emphasis mine)

Do you have a Hymenaeus or Philetus in your life? Maybe you married one. People who twist your words to fit their narrative, even convincing others you're not to be trusted.

Or, have you experienced times when even your prayer and kindness, far from cutting down the problems, have seemed only to worsen them?

That's what Paul experienced. And for him, there was more:

> Do your best to come to me soon. For Demas, in love with this present world, has deserted me and gone to Thessalonica. Crescens has gone to Galatia, Titus to Dalmatia. Luke alone is with me. . . . Alexander the coppersmith did me great harm; the Lord will repay him according to his deeds. . . . At my first defense *no one came to stand by me, but all deserted me.* (2 Tim. 4:9–10, 14, 16, emphasis mine)

After the first few of these instances, I would've had enough. But the names just roll on for Paul—Demas, Crescens, Titus. Only Luke was left. Finally the apostle hit bottom: "No one came to stand by me, but all deserted me" (v. 16). In one of the darkest moments, when his life was under indescribable assault, Paul stood alone. Then he died.

None of us signs up for a desertion-plagued existence. No one anticipates marrying into a life that ends like Paul's did. It's the exact opposite of what we think the Christian life should be! It's all so humiliating, so unresolved, so . . . open-ended. If we're in a Christian marriage and applying the gospel to our lives, we assume things will resolve. Confusing trauma will be replaced by tidy closure.

But what do you do if you have a life or a marriage more like Paul's final days . . . filled with unresolved relational grief . . . awash in complexity? No tidy bows. No resolution. No closure.

Seriously, how do we know if we're living a life of faith or if we've been taken captive by *misguided expectations* for closure? Here are three clues for misguided expectations.

## Captivity Clue #1: I'm Looking for Peace outside of Faith

- Ten years, still no improvement with your in-laws.
- You've spoken to your spouse countless times and even sought counseling, but changes in your marriage are barely discernable.
- You wanted to talk to your mom about what happened to you growing up, but now she has passed.
- Your spouse gets angry, flips the chill switch for a few days, then moves on without ever discussing their hurt or offense.

All of these examples share one similarity: there's no closure, no resolution, no apologies, no forgiveness, not even "let bygones be bygones."

Where do you find peace? We know we're called to be men and women of faith, but what does this mean?

In Hebrews 11, we're treated to a whirlwind tour of the Hall of Faith. We encounter Abel, Enoch, Noah, Jacob, Moses, and a host of other faith heroes—including a couple surprise cameos, as we discussed in chapter 8. Tucked indiscriminately within this chapter are some astonishing words regarding these faith heroes: "These all died in faith, not having received the things promised" (v. 13). Think about this. Every one of the heroes listed in Hebrews 11 died holding on to unfulfilled promises and unsatisfied dreams. They died without closure.

Hebrews teaches that we're called to trust God in the midst of a maddeningly fractured, open-ended, closure-less world. Friends, we have to face it: *closure is overrated.* God doesn't promise it, and we don't find peace by getting ultimate answers. We find peace only by clinging to a good God in the midst of perplexing pain.

You're called to be a husband who trusts God's providence, even when you don't understand why your wife's depression doesn't resolve. You're called to be a woman who stands in faith, despite the fact that your husband is trapped in addiction. Don't misunderstand me. You're not called to settle for sinful behavior or to resign yourself to a life with no hope for change. On the contrary, you're called to a faith that trusts God to transform your spouse *and* rests contentedly in his timetable.

> We don't find peace by getting ultimate answers. We find peace only by clinging to a good God in the midst of perplexing pain.

We are called to escape this captivity. To stand emancipated by the reality that true peace can't be dictated by people. Peace has to be found outside the illusion of closure.

In a fallen world filled with complex relationships, the true heroes are those who can see that lasting peace is only found beyond the grave.

I once read Lyle Dorsett's biography of A. W. Tozer. Tozer was a spiritual giant—a man of spectacular faith, incredible insight, and compelling godliness. But Tozer neglected his wife, Ada, and their family in some pretty stunning ways. Apparently, Tozer was far more heavenly minded than marriage minded. He would travel extensively and often left Ada alone. There's clear evidence that he ignored his family's material needs. He died and left his wife penniless.

After Tozer's death, Ada remarried a man named Leonard Odam. Dorsett writes of a poignant moment when Ada was asked to describe her life with her new husband. "I have never been happier in my life," Ada observed. "Aiden [Tozer] loved Jesus Christ, but Leonard Odam loves me."[1]

A. W. Tozer, a remarkably holy preacher and powerful writer, was a sinner, and his sin shaped his wife's remembrance of his love. Ada never resolved the disconnect between the spiritual giant of a preacher and the husband who seemed to love ministry more than her. Her understanding of their marriage wasn't bundled up into a neat package for her. How was she supposed to interpret all those years of being married to a godly man who never came alive in this one important area? How does a wife move forward? From where does she get resolution? Where does she find peace?

Think about your own life.

What moves a beleaguered wife forward? What kick-starts a baffled husband? It's a vital question. The longing to make sense out of the absurd twists in our journey can be pretty beguiling. We feel we'll be made whole through interpretation, apologies, restoration, nostalgia, or the return to a flourishing past. But what's often happening is that we are losing our appetite for trusting God. By looking for something from others, we subtly marginalize God.

When held captive by a craving for closure, we need a faith rooted in God's faithfulness. And his faithfulness can't be measured by

1. Lyle Dorsett, *A Passion for God: The Spiritual Journey of A. W. Tozer* (Chicago: Moody, 2008), 160.

whether we have a eureka moment of meaning. Marriage does not come with a label that says, "If resolution does not appear, return immediately for full refund." God's faithfulness can't be measured by whether we have an epiphany about what he's doing through our unresolved pain. Faith does not need a defined outcome so that God can be vindicated or understood.

> When held captive by a craving for closure, we need a faith rooted in God's faithfulness.

Faith, by contrast, is "the conviction of things not seen" (Heb. 11:1). This is the ground Paul finally set his feet on. After his long list of unresolved relationships, he writes:

> But the Lord stood at my side and strengthened me, so that through me the message might be fully proclaimed and all the Gentiles might hear it. So I was rescued from the lion's mouth. The Lord will rescue me from every evil deed and bring me safely into his heavenly kingdom. (2 Tim. 4:17–18)

## Captivity Clue #2: In the Absence of Closure, I've Become a Cynic

"Whatever!" Few words capture our culture of contempt more than this prickly exclamation. We hear it often: a student's eye-rolling response to her teacher's direction; an employee's muttered protest when told to get back to work; a harried mom's exasperated murmur when her husband says he can't pick up the kids.

"Whatever" is a verbal wave of dismissal. It's the armor of apathy that shields our heart from the hassle of other people's agendas.

The Bible says the words we speak overflow from our hearts (Luke 6:45). When we've been denied closure, our hearts often voice "Whatever!" It's hostility with a harness—a subtle, irritated, pouting resentment. "Whatever" often betrays a cynical heart—one growing hard because it can't understand why its desires have been denied. The word may be loud or lazy, strong or subtle, bold or brittle, but its cool detachment masks a thousand disillusioned slights. When our pessimism grows dark, a cynic is born.

What exactly is cynicism? Cynicism "sees" through the appearance of good and unmasks the "bad" behind it. I enclosed "sees" and "bad" in quotation marks, because a cynical person will see the worst possibility whether it's there or not. Cynicism turns *Saturday Night Live* into a way of life. Everything is a joke and everyone is an idiot. All of life becomes a sarcastic punch line.

Cynicism is where our unbelief and bitterness disguise themselves as discernment.

When faith gets tired of waiting for resolution or interpretation, a heart can begin to see the worst. It grows cynical.

Sonya has become a cynic. She doesn't see it, but she occasionally smells the fruit. Sonya and Sam wanted kids. In fact, "want" doesn't begin to describe the depth of their desires. They both came from large families and married with dreams of a bustling home. Yet, as each year passed, the kids never came.

Eventually Sonya stopped asking God. She was burnt out from the experience of expecting but not receiving. What did her barrenness mean? She wanted to know. She wanted to understand. She wondered whether they should pull the trigger on adoption. The lack of answers became an open wound in her soul. Sonya stopped attending the many baby showers in the church. She would come home and recount them for Sam with a tone tinged with contempt. As time continued, Sonya would just roll her eyes at the announcement of another pregnancy. Turning to Sam, she would whisper a witty criticism of the couple, one that barely concealed her struggling heart. But Sam knew something was wasting away within.

Why do we give in to cynicism? Cynicism is subtle scoffing; it's a way of protecting ourselves from disappointment and pain. Let's face it. There are times when marriage will disappoint all of us. It's true even in the best marriages. We marry with the assumption that we are enjoying a foretaste of heaven, then live rocked by how earthly marriage becomes. "How would you answer the questions, 'Do I live for heaven?' or 'Do I live demanding that life be like heaven?'" asks Dan Allender. "Your answers will determine what you will spend your life fighting for." [2]

Christians who assume they're marrying into some version of heaven become cynical when their marriage falls to earth.

## Captivity Clue #3: Things Will Never Go Wrong If I Just Get It Right

I came to faith in the late 1970s, in a strain of Christianity that believed we were living in a unique end-times period where God was restoring his church. We believed the church was heading back toward Acts 2 living—community, prayer, and power. People would be healed. Divorce would never happen. Conflict would always be resolved. We felt that we were ushering in an expression of Christianity where we could finally get things right.

There are many blessings I carried away from that season. But one incontrovertible yet ill-conceived conviction remained wedged for years deep within my soul: *God's people applying God's Word could overcome any problem.* Here's another way to say it: "If we apply God's truth correctly and just do things right, then things will go right." Getting things right seemed to be our antidote for fallenness. Correct practice would always deliver closure. Life would be like a good Tom Hanks film. In the end, things would always resolve. *If* I just get it right.

This false belief impacted Kimm's and my approach to marriage: "If we can just date regularly, live transparently, confess sincerely, and submit humbly, then we can avoid the mistakes of the past. We can get it right."

Unsurprisingly, this slice of deterministic obedience affected our parenting too. We thought being faithful parents would determine the spiritual health of our kids: "If I obey the Bible, discipline

2. Dan B. Allender and Tremper Longman III, *Bold Love* (Colorado Springs: NavPress, 1992), 140.

consistently, and push the catechism, then my kids will look good on earth and be present in heaven."

No parent in our world would have said it out loud, but it became a form of "justification by parenting." Such legalism smuggles in a confidence that God rewards faithful parents with obedient, converted kids—proportionally to what we deserve. *I've put in serious work, so I deserve impressive kids!*

We also flipped it. If the gospel of determinism is true, then wayward people are the result of the faults and flaws of others. If one spouse is spinning out of control, the other is just reaping what they've sowed.

I'm not suggesting leadership, godliness, or good parenting don't matter. Godly parenting, for instance, influences children positively and bad parenting influences them negatively. But the key word is *influence*. In marriage and parenting, too many Christians unwittingly confuse influence with guaranteed results. This assumption takes God, the world's brokenness, and the human will out of the equation. As Russell Moore writes:

> Something has gone terribly wrong when a Christian feels she must protect herself from her church, for fear that her daughter's spiritual crisis will be discussed as part of a debate over whether she should have breastfed longer or whether they should have chosen homeschooling over public school. That's especially true when literally every family in Scripture, without exception, has prodigals, including that of God the Father.[3]

We're not masters of our own destiny, of our spouse's destiny, or of our children's destinies. As Moore observes, "God is the *perfect* Father and yet still has wayward children (Rom. 3:23; Luke 15:11–32). What could possibly make us think that such could never be part of our story?"[4]

3. Russell Moore, *The Storm-Tossed Family: How the Cross Reshapes the Home* (Nashville: B&H, 2018), 16–17.
4. Moore, *The Storm-Tossed Family*, 16–17.

The truth is that fallenness is inescapable. Time revealed this truth to us and our church. Teenagers rebelled. Marriages got hard. Life happened. We learned a painful lesson: our obedience and Christian lifestyle do not guarantee immediate or predetermined results. The belief that "If I get it right, things will never go wrong" turned out to be embarrassingly misguided. So many things remain unfixed and open-ended in this life.

> We're not masters of our own destiny, of our spouse's destiny, or of our children's destinies.

The married couple who believes "things will never go wrong if we just get it right" has set themselves up for disappointment—and worse. Clinging to such deterministic beliefs bears bad fruit. It can make us Pharisees when things go well and leave us oppressed when things don't.

## Christ Sets the Captives Free

Yes, the news sounds discouraging—a broken world leaves life open-ended. It is often bad news. People often do get hurt. And remain hurt. One cannot always look for the silver lining, as sometimes there is none. But there is news that has hope attached to it. And it has hope because of God, who attaches the hope. God always has a good plan wrapped up in his perfect purposes. And while closure may elude us in the present, we have it anchored in far more important places.

### The Past!

The gospel is glorious because it represents God's closure on the most important open-ended matters of the universe: the tragedy of our sin and our separation from a holy God. In Christ, we have resolution on the crisis of sin, and we hope for the day when all will be made right. When a lack of resolution darkens the present, we can go back to what Christ accomplished on Golgotha and remember "It is finished!" Sweet closure has been achieved.

Sure, all of our life is not wrapped up tight. There are areas where, like Paul, our relational world remains painfully open-ended. Maybe it's a former spouse, an old friend, even someone in the family. We've tried, but we just aren't reconciled in the way we desire. It's so good to remember that, because of Christ, you already possess the reconciliation that matters most.

We grieve unreconciled relationships. We really do. They're among the most difficult burdens to bear in this world. But where there is a disproportionate impact that lingers too long and colors our world with gloom, might it be that the approval of that person or group mattered more than it should? Remember, as a believer you wake up every morning with your most important relationship intact.

We hope for the broken relationship to be mended, for the complicated situation to be resolved. But we don't *need* it to be. By loving me enough to die for my sins, Christ has met my deepest need.

### The Future!

But there's more good news. Our hope doesn't simply remain tucked away in the past. Lift your eyes to see a future coming! It carries the closure that presently eludes you. The anticipation of a new heaven and new earth reminds us that unresolved conflicts, marriage challenges, betrayal, injustice, and broken relationships are temporary pains. Resolution is speeding toward you with the passing of every moment of every day. People who may cross the street to avoid the awkwardness of greeting you will soon weep for joy at the sight of you in the world to come. Every bad seed with a heart bent toward evil will be either converted or condemned. The pleasure of unending joy will replace the pain of unresolved questions.

Only a certain future like this can temper our momentary grievances. In a surprising twist, though, you will learn how God used those scars to help you endure in ways you never dreamed.

Yes, closure will come. But for the moment, it's overrated.

# Defining Moment #10:
## When You Learn Closure Is Overrated

When we enter marriage, most of us assume that if we apply the gospel to our lives, we can live a life where things resolve—where trauma can be replaced by tidy closure. But what do you do if you have a life or marriage filled with unresolved relational grief?

| | The Moment | Our Response |
|---|---|---|
| **The Decision for Truth** | Will I allow a lack of resolution to hold me captive and become an oppressive burden for our marriage? | Or will I recognize that God's kingdom is present but not yet consummated—that salvation has come even while brokenness and death persist? |
| **The Cost Required** | Will I believe that getting things right is the antidote for fallenness? | Or will I trust that the only one who gets things right is Jesus, who freely gives his righteousness to us despite our failures? |
| **The God-Exalting Opportunity** | Will I need immediate change or immediate answers in order to experience peace? | Or will I trust God's providence over our broken life, persisting in faith even when answers and transformation elude us? |
| **The Way It Grows the Soul** | Will I protect myself from disappointment and pain at all costs? | Or will I believe that the reconciliation we most need has already been won for us in Christ, even when I can't see it in our circumstances? |
| **The Way It Sets Our Destination** | Will I become cynical, seeing the worst in every situation whether it's there or not? | Or will I lift my eyes away from temporary realities to the certainty of a restored future in the new heaven and new earth? |

# When Grace Conquers Your Wasted Moments: *The Death of Ivan Ilych*

Have you ever wasted an afternoon? Come on, be honest. We all have. On some level, we're all binge-watching, class-cutting, work-skipping types who can fess up to a little wasted time. We've all logged some absences. Yet even despite your catalog of legitimate regrets, "waste" probably isn't at the center of your story.

But what if it was? What if true clarity on how to live and love only arrived with your final gasps?

## Introducing Ivan

Count Leo Tolstoy (1828–1910) was born into an affluent, blue-blooded Russian family. Leo had an aristocratic start. His family dished privileges his way, until in his forties he experienced a crisis of conscience followed by a spiritual awakening. Most historians believe this was a genuine conversion to Christ marked by monastic practices and a passionate advocacy for the poor.

Besides writing the hefty *War and Peace*, one of Russia's greatest novels, Tolstoy wrote *The Death of Ivan Ilych*, a smaller book about an ordinary, middle-class Russian judge. Ivan Ilych is distinguished by nothing but a settled ambivalence toward the world outside. He is competent, ambitious, agreeable to a fault, and laced with the kind of vanity that fuels self-obsession. In other words, he's a calculating soul who spends his career striving to get ahead.

To Ivan, life is a stage where one's performance is measured by the impression left on others. The books he reads, the attire he wears, his possessions, the countenance he contrives—everything about Ivan conforms to the correct social conventions. All become well-placed pillars, propping up his delusions of grandeur.

Now, Ivan Ilych is not without commendable qualities. He is intelligent, dutiful, and hospitable. Yet his soul is morally shallow—hardly deep enough to buoy any interests but his own. In a world where each sunrise beams with mystery and complexity, Ivan avoids the light, content to dwell in the gray twilight of an unexamined life. Thus, Ivan presents a textbook example of a wasted life, the horror of which comes not from evil but from *ambivalence* toward his wife, his family, and others.

Ivan is not merely a man; he is a symbol of life lived without God—the epic consequence of a distracted existence. "Ivan Ilych's life," Tolstoy begins, "had been most simple and most ordinary and therefore most terrible."[1]

When does an ordinary and simple life become terrible? Tolstoy's answer: when that ordinary and simple life is wasted on a propped-up delusion of self.

Tolstoy illustrates Ivan's trifling existence most clearly in the rhythms of his marriage. Ivan's wife is Praskovya Fyodorovna

1. Leo Tolstoy, *The Death of Ivan Ilych*, trans. Aylmer and Louise Maude, Oxford World Classics 432 (London: Oxford University Press, 1935), 11. All excerpts quoted in this chapter are in the public domain.

Golovina, a vacuous character who meets Ivan's thin morality with her own weightless worldview. Their marriage is a coalition of convenience.... until it isn't. Initially decorative to Ivan's image, what we might call a "trophy wife" today, Praskovya slowly becomes an impediment to Ivan's comfort, a shrill disruptor of his peace. "His wife, without any reason," as Ivan expresses it to himself, "began to disturb the pleasure and propriety of their life."[2] She demands Ivan's attention, finds fault with the way he treats her, grows jealous without cause, and sometimes makes "coarse and ill-mannered scenes."[3]

> Ivan is not merely a man; he is a symbol of life lived without God—the epic consequence of a distracted existence.

For Ivan, a guy whose life is more skimmed than scrutinized, Praskovya's behavior becomes intolerable. So he withdraws and creates a cozy domain outside the reach of his wife's annoying moods and irksome demands.

It is from this island place—with Ivan isolated, Praskovya contained, their marriage a mere ceremonial association—that Count Tolstoy's story sets sail. But the destination of his story is Ivan's final breaths—the arrival of his death.

## A Life of Regrets

One day Ivan detects a pain in his side. As an individual unaccustomed to discomfort, the presence of pain buries him under a landslide of self-pity. His mind spins inward and downward as his world shrinks to the agony of his aches. The illness takes control and, though undiagnosed, becomes inexplicably fatal . . . simply because Ivan believes it will be.

Ivan's physical decline pushes him quite unexpectedly toward the threshold of moral reflection. From there he steps slowly and

2. Tolstoy, *The Death of Ivan Ilych*, 18.
3. Tolstoy, *The Death of Ivan Ilych*, 18.

hesitantly toward unexplored terrain. In one episode of self-inflicted suffering, Ivan experiences a flash of moral clarity:

> "It is as if I had been going downhill while I imagined I was going up. And that is really what it was. I was going up in public opinion, but to the same extent life was ebbing away from me. And now it is all done and there is only death."[4]

For Ivan, death clears the mind. His final hour becomes his defining moment, marked by the arrival of an anguished question: *What if my whole life has been wrong?*

To be human is to be fallen. We are not divine but damaged, not infallible but flawed, not boundless but broken. To be alive is to wrestle with regret. *Did I marry the wrong person? Did I take the wrong job? Did I miss my calling? Did I parent too selfishly? Did I live too lazily?*

> To be human is to be fallen. We are not divine but damaged, not infallible but flawed, not boundless but broken. To be alive is to wrestle with regret.

Through Ivan Ilych, Count Tolstoy invites us to consider this delicate but perennial problem. Ivan seemingly asks: *Now that I'm brutally honest and my real problems sharpen in clarity, is it too late to resolve those problems? If my entire life has gone wrong, and my marriage has been wrong, can it be made right again? Is there hope for someone who's neglected decisions for truth and allowed the defining moments to pass? Can my largest failures at critical junctures be overcome?*

## The Sting of Death

Death is never a mere "passing." It's what happens when judgment meets fallenness. For those who glide over the smaller griefs, death becomes a violent accounting, a bracing moment where

4. Tolstoy, *The Death of Ivan Ilych*, 64.

the hurricane of truth makes landfall. If life is a foolish man's house, the bare truth that comes at death levels the fool. The soul-searching questions can become Category 5 winds, catastrophic when they remain unanswered. Ivan stands helpless before the destructive gales of accusation as his final moments fill with unshielded agony:

> It occurred to him that what had appeared perfectly impossible before, namely that he had not spent his life as he should have done, might after all be true. It occurred to him that his scarcely perceptible attempts to struggle against what was considered good by the most highly placed people, those scarcely noticeable impulses which he had immediately suppressed, might have been the real thing, and all the rest false. And his professional duties and the whole arrangement of his life and of his family, and all his social and official interests, might all have been false. He tried to defend all those things to himself and suddenly felt the weakness of what he was defending. There was nothing to defend.
>
> "But if that is so," he said to himself, "and I am leaving this life with the consciousness that I have lost all that was given me and it is impossible to rectify it—what then?"[5]

With no answer, Ivan is gripped by a foreboding sense of gloom. He's despondent. Misery chews his soul. As the man's life drains from his frame, questions long buried begin to surface like bodies in a dried-up river basin. Still, there are no answers.

Then, in an uncharacteristic display of concern, Ivan's wife Praskovya begs for him to take communion. It's the desperate appeal of an abandoned wife for the lost soul of her husband.

Ivan agrees—maybe just to appease her. But in that moment, a flash of truth bursts. Ivan has a moment of lucidity, a defining moment. As the curtain of his life closes, Ivan sees that his soul has been contorted, corrupted, and hopelessly lost.

5. Tolstoy, *The Death of Ivan Ilych*, 69.

My friends, pity the man who sees his soul without the protection of an advocate or mediator! As the reality of a wasted marriage and a wasted life crashes in on his conscience, Ivan begins to scream:

> From that moment the screaming began that continued for three days, and it was so terrible that one could not hear it through two closed doors without horror. At the moment he answered his wife he realized that he was lost, that there was no return, that the end had come, the very end, and his doubts were still unsolved and remained doubts.
> "Oh! Oh! Oh!" he cried in various intonations. . . .
> For three whole days, during which time did not exist for him, he struggled. . . . He struggled as a man condemned to death struggles in the hands of the executioner, knowing that he cannot save himself. And every moment he felt that despite all his efforts he was drawing nearer and nearer to what terrified him. . . . [His previous] justification of his life held him fast and prevented his moving forward, and it caused him most torment of all.[6]

Let's pause, take a breath, and reconsider this scene. We are now perched along the rail, overlooking Ivan's darkest moment. We can trace the neural pathways of his tortured and frantic mind as the dreadful truth surfaces. The notion of a wasted life is too horrifying to accept, so Ivan's conscience (and perhaps his flesh) works overtime, pillaging the past and searching in vain for a way to justify himself. A dying man in his most significant moment desperately needs immunity for his decisions, his indulgences, and his dispositions. Buried deeply in Ivan—and really, in us all—is a defense attorney who denies our culpability and desperately searches for evidence to rationalize thousands of self-obsessed acts and omissions.

> Buried deeply in us all is a defense attorney who denies our culpability and desperately searches for evidence to rationalize thousands of self-obsessed acts and omissions.

6. Tolstoy, *The Death of Ivan Ilych*, 71.

But no such advocate is found. Ivan stands accused, guilty, and deserving of death. He sees his trifling life. He sees beneath it all a wasteland of barren vanity.

Ivan lies dying, utterly defeated—broken up by life in a broken-down world. The condemnation escalates as the revelation of his self-justification triggers "the most tormenting moment of all." The road to hell is paved with people who, on the surface, seem to have ordinary lives. But when you dig below, you discover bad motives and a myriad of terrible choices. This is Ivan Ilych's life—simple, ordinary, and *terrible*. Ivan lies suspended between two worlds, a culpable collaborator to his own demise.

> What can be done for a man whose dying breaths are haunted by wasted relationships, a wasted marriage, and a wasted life?

Is he beyond the reach of help? More importantly, are you? What can be done for a man whose dying breaths are haunted by wasted relationships, a wasted marriage, and a wasted life?

## The Redefining Power of Grace

He too hung suspended between two worlds, this thief nailed to a cross. Crucified alongside him were two others. One was a fool dying for his crimes. The other was God. Three men, pinned to three trees, all in the throes of death and encountering defining moments where, like Ivan, their words revealed their hearts.

"Are you not the Christ?" the fool screamed. "Save yourself and us!" (Luke 23:39). In the mouth of a fool, those words mean "Forget yourself and save me!" The trouble with fools is they don't see God (Ps. 53:1), even when he's hanging right next to them. This thief died reviling God (Matt. 27:44). His final moment sealed his fate.

The other thief also hung as a hardened criminal, but he softened in death. This man was a first-century Ivan Ilych nailed to a tree. But unlike Ivan, we get no glimpse into his final thoughts. Only his words to his crucified companions are preserved. Yet they display the width, breadth, and depth of God's grace.

First, he speaks to the fool: "Do you not fear God, since you are under the same sentence of condemnation? And we indeed justly, for we are receiving the due reward of our deeds; but this man has done nothing wrong" (Luke 23:40–41).

> Can Jesus save someone from the just penalty of a wasted life?

Then he speaks to the Savior: "Jesus, remember me when you come into your kingdom" (23:42).

Though this thief bore the consequences of wasted criminal years, the grace he received in his final moments redefined his life. "Truly, I say to you," Jesus whispered to him, "today you will be with me in paradise" (23:43).

Is grace really powerful enough to snatch someone from the consequences of a life of crime, insanity, and absurd, self-centered stupidity? Can Jesus save someone from the just penalty of a wasted life?

Or perhaps the question we really need to answer is, *Should* he?

## Irrational Grace

Jesus told a parable about laborers hired for the day. The master hired workers for his vineyard at the beginning of the day and promised a denarius, a good day's wage. Then the master kept hiring workers as the day went on, even bringing in a group just an hour before the workday ended. When the whistle blew, the foreman gathered all the workers and paid the last ones who had been hired a denarius—the full day's wage! Seeing this, the ones hired earlier in the day expected a bonus; they had, after all, worked longer and harder.

It didn't happen. The foreman paid each worker exactly as arranged when they were hired—one denarius.

The worked-all-day dudes grumbled. They thought the master had acted unjustly. They felt they deserved more. Equal pay for unequal work appeared to be an injustice, a fundamentally unfair compensation policy. "But [the master] replied to one of them, 'Friend, I am doing you no wrong. Did you not agree with me for a denarius? Take what belongs to you and go. I choose to give to this last worker as I give to you. Am I not allowed to do what I choose with what belongs to me? Or do you begrudge my generosity?'" (Matt. 20:13–16).

How we see the master in this parable says much about our grasp of grace. Did those who worked all day deserve more than was promised? Did the master's generosity toward the partial-day guys obligate him to change everyone's pay scale? The Workers Union might say yes. What do you say?

With this story, Jesus exposes our entitled hearts. We ever scan the fields for the worker who seems less deserving, to make a case for why we deserve more. We are moral money-changers, weakening the value of grace by converting it back to the currency of our own merit. The worked-all-day guys compare themselves to the others and conclude they deserve more. But God's generosity toward some is not his injustice toward others.

> God's generosity toward some is not his injustice toward others.

God flipped the script. In Christ, the last is first and the first is last. He gives the same grace regardless of the hours worked. So grace snatches a dying thief from the flames and delivers him straight into paradise. It is the way God can deal with a wasted life. Is there a part of you that begrudges the thief for that mercy?

## When Waste Meets Grace

This is why I love the story of Ivan Ilych. His marriage is wasted. His life is wasted. He deserves eternal consequences. The pathetic narcissist is a dying, miserable man. How would I feel about him getting generosity that he doesn't deserve?

Tolstoy's story concludes with Ivan's final defining moment:

> Suddenly some force struck him in the chest and side, making it still harder to breathe, and he fell through [a] hole and there at the bottom was a light. What had happened to him was like the sensation one sometimes experiences in a railway carriage when one thinks one is going backwards while one is really going forwards and suddenly becomes aware of the real direction.
>
> "Yes, it was all not the right thing," he said to himself, "but that's no matter. It can be done. But what *is* the right thing?" he asked himself, and suddenly grew quiet.
>
> This occurred at the end of the third day, two hours before his death. Just then his schoolboy son had crept softly in and gone up to the bedside. The dying man was still screaming desperately and waving his arms. His hand fell on the boy's head, and the boy caught it, pressed it to his lips, and began to cry.
>
> At that very moment Ivan Ilych fell through and caught sight of the light, and it was revealed to him that though his life had not been what it should have been, this could still be rectified. He asked himself, "What is the right thing?" and grew still, listening.[7]

Something unexpected happens. Grace appears at the unforgiving bottom of a wasted life. Ivan grows still, perhaps for the first time in his life. He lies prostrate—thinking, listening, and asking, *What is the right thing?*

In the deepest hole of human existence, God is present. Like the thief whispering, "Will you remember me when you come into your kingdom?" (Luke 23:42), God supplies Ivan with the right request, and by grace he shows him the way to climb. Sometimes the ladder comes from the most unexpected places:

7. Tolstoy, *The Death of Ivan Ilych*, 72.

Then [Ivan Ilych] felt that someone was kissing his hand. He opened his eyes, looked at his son, and felt sorry for him. His wife came up to him and he glanced at her. She was gazing at him open-mouthed, with undried tears on her nose and cheek and a despairing look on her face. He felt sorry for her too.

"Yes, I am making them wretched," he thought. "They are sorry, but it will be better for them when I die." He wished to say this but had not the strength to utter it. "Besides, why speak? I must act," he thought. With a look at his wife he indicated his son and said: "Take him away . . . sorry for him . . . sorry for you too. . . ." He tried to add, "forgive me," but said "forego" and waved his hand, knowing that He whose understanding mattered would understand.

And suddenly it grew clear to him that what had been oppressing him and would not leave him was all dropping away at once from two sides, from ten sides, and from all sides. He was sorry for them, [and] he must act so as not to hurt them: release them and free himself from these sufferings. "How good and how simple!" he thought. "And the pain?" he asked himself. "What has become of it? Where are you, pain?"

He turned his attention to it.

"Yes, here it is. Well, what of it? Let the pain be."[8]

When grace comes, pain shrinks back to its proper size. Suffering is always serious and intensely significant, but it need not define us. As Ivan encounters God's grace, he temporarily misplaces his pain. Ivan's condition isn't changed, but his pain—which in Tolstoy's hands becomes a metaphor for Ivan's self-love—no longer reigns supreme over his soul. Ivan's idol has been dethroned; God's presence takes command. Ivan's wife comes into focus; a new love is born. And under love's new dominion, fear would not reign.

> In the deepest hole of human existence, God is present.

8. Tolstoy, *The Death of Ivan Ilych*, 72–73.

"And death . . . where is it?"

He sought his former accustomed fear of death and did not find it. "Where is it? What death?" There was no fear because there was no death.

In place of death there was light.

"So that's what it is!" he suddenly exclaimed aloud. "What joy!"

To him all this happened in a single instant, and the meaning of that instant did not change. For those present his agony continued for another two hours. Something rattled in his throat, his emaciated body twitched, then the gasping and rattle became less and less frequent.

"It is finished!" said someone near him.

He heard these words and repeated them in his soul.

"Death is finished," he said to himself. "It is no more!"

He drew in a breath, stopped in the midst of a sigh, stretched out, and died.[9]

Where grace goes to war, grace wins. The very power needed to repent comes from the One who loves to forgive (Eph. 2:8). As grace peels back the fingers of terror choking his heart, Ivan Ilych finds this to be true. Though he still walks "through the valley of the shadow of death," Ivan fears no evil. God is now with him. God comforts him (Ps. 23:4–5). God emancipates him from his fears (Heb. 2:15). Indeed, grace robbed death of its power over a wasted life. "O death, where is your victory? O death, where is your sting?" (1 Cor. 15:55).

> Suffering is always serious and intensely significant, but it need not define us.

Ivan's final words, "Death is finished," are barely audible. But they're present enough to reveal that his life will be covered by the death of another, One whose final words were spoken from a blood-spattered cross at Golgotha—the *ultimate* defining moment. Jesus lived a perfect life to emancipate us from the prison of a wasted life.

9. Tolstoy, *The Death of Ivan Ilych*, 73.

Grace wins. In his final gasp, Ivan whispers, "[Death] is no more." The fear, pain, and crushing condemnation of a life spent at the altar of Ivan evaporate under the blazing sunrise of a newfound affection for his wife and son. When Ivan hung suspended over the flaming fires of hell, Christ swooped in, snatched him up, and carried him to safety.

> Jesus lived a perfect life to emancipate us from the prison of a wasted life.

## Where Grace Wins, Waste Loses

It's possible, I suppose, to distort Count Tolstoy's intent in writing this tale. Grace that saves a soul only moments before death could be seen as grace that winks at a wasted life. But Ivan Ilych's story is not an invitation to squander your life in anticipation of a last-minute reprieve. In fact, Tolstoy anticipates this misapplication by opening the novella with Ivan's funeral and describing his frozen, pale features: "Besides this there was in that expression a reproach and a warning to the living."[10]

The drama of Ivan's death *is* a warning. Tolstoy invites us to consider our lives, our marriages, our parenting. Misplaced love, particularly an inordinate self-love, comes at a staggering moral cost. Ivan's missed opportunities should tutor us.

What about you? What if, looking back at your life, you only see missed opportunities? What if much of your married life has been a waste? Even then, your sin is not the final word. Christ is greater than your wasted decisions and willful self-pity. Undeserved grace for a wasted life shouldn't merely stir your gratitude; it should fire your ambition to change. Grace stands ready to forgive your past and reorient your perspective in at least three practical ways:

- *First, grace contends for our holiness, especially in marriage.* Earlier in this book, I wrote about how marriage

10. Tolstoy, *The Death of Ivan Ilych*, 5.

reveals our weakness. Sometimes God uses our spouse's brokenness to expose our selfishness. Ivan blamed his many problems on Praskovya's coarseness, need for attention, and ill manners. He couldn't see that the discomfort brought by her rough edges might be a means for his growth. God always sends grace to train us in holiness (Titus 2:14). A grace perspective, then, allows us to treasure our spouse as God's gift to help us change. At the end, even Ivan Ilych found grace through his wife's concern for his lost soul. Her appeal for him to receive communion was the trigger that fired him toward Christ. He'd only find salvation at the end of himself. Grace always works this way. First it exposes our brokenness, then it shows us our need for help.

- *Second, grace intercepts our isolation and moves us to confession.* Ivan had cut himself off from his wife and son. He'd run from God like Jonah, the prodigal prophet, sailing toward Tarshish. Ivan's family was his long-neglected Nineveh. He got there eventually, but it wasn't a great fish or a withered vine that softened his heart. In the end, his son's touch worked empathy and compassion within. Ivan's last breaths were used to pursue forgiveness, peace, and reconciliation with his family. Like Ivan, are you running from God right now? Admitting it may actually trigger your defining moment. There's no need to wait until death to confess sin and find peace. Don't be afraid, and don't feel condemned. Remember, your sin is not the final word. There is One who is greater than your wasted decisions and willful indulgences. He stands ready to forgive your past and reorient your present. He stands ready to redefine your life so that you may be ready for your final defining moment.

- *Finally, grace wins so we can put aside our performance.* So much of Ivan's life was spent performing for others and indulging his ambitions at the expense of true priorities. He wasted his relationships to the point where he'd become more of a burden on his family than a blessing. He saw this at the end and it was crushing. But Ivan's failures didn't define his destiny. Ultimately, his life was defined by One who performed for him. As he died, he heard someone say, "It is finished." These words are a symbolic echo of Christ's words on the cross, and Ivan heard them in exactly that way. They stoked his inner joy and delight. Ivan had become like Christ in his death, and this gave him confidence that somehow he'd be like Christ in the resurrection (Phil. 3:10–11). Though his body died, inwardly he was renewed (2 Cor. 4:16). Tolstoy tells us, "He heard these words and repeated them in his soul. 'Death is finished,' he said to himself. 'It is no more!'"[11]

## This Defining Moment

Throughout this book, we've explored defining moments common to aging marriages. Each presents a decision for truth, points to a path forward, and determines a new direction. Each moment is important, but there is a defining moment coming that has far greater importance. Though it's not on our calendar, it's a future appointment we all share. It is the moment we meet God and he reveals the true aim of our life and the real object of our love. It is *God's* defining moment when, after we've spent our life defining ourselves before others, God finally defines us before all of heaven. In that moment we live not wasted but vanquished by grace forevermore.

Because Christ's grace contends for our holiness—because grace intercepts our isolation and moves us to peace—we can face this coming day knowing that, through faith in Christ, we'll

11. Tolstoy, *The Death of Ivan Ilych,* 73.

hear words of grace: "Well done, good and faithful servant. You have been faithful over a little; I will set you over much. Enter into the joy of your master" (Matt. 25:23).

Because grace wins, friends, you can face your final moments with confidence and hope.

> Now to him who is able to keep you from stumbling and to present you blameless before the presence of his glory with great joy, to the only God, our Savior, through Jesus Christ our Lord, be glory, majesty, dominion, and authority, before all time and now and forever. Amen. (Jude 24–25)

# Acknowledgments

For some gifted souls, writing flows from finding private space and coaxing their inner author outside to play in the field of words. I admire those folks. I really do. But that's not me. My inner author prefers community. In fact, I need community to produce anything worth reading. It takes a village for me to write a book.

Let me introduce you to my village, without whom this project would not exist.

Thanks to Brian and the team at Baker Books. They caught a vision to publish a sequel to *When Sinners Say "I Do,"* and then they labored diligently to see it come to fruition.

Jared Kennedy, thank you! Your sharp mind, keen grammatical eye, and grade-A editorial skills left their imprint on every chapter. I'm also grateful to Matt Smethurst, who agreed to use his unwavering talent to make this a better book. Chapter 8—"the sex chapter"—stalled until Pete Greasley helped me infuse it with some clarity. Stay ornery, my friend. It's beautiful.

Thank you to the host of readers who graciously agreed to review the book and who offered insights on its strengths and weaknesses and made suggestions for how to improve it. My unending thanks go out to my dear wife Kimm, Lou and Whitney Angelo, Todd Augustine, Orlando Cabrera, Elyse Fitzpatrick, Ronnie

Martin, Chris Minott, John and Cindy Schmidler, and our traveling companions, John and Margie Stewart. A thousand apologies if my aging mind has overlooked any other helpful villagers.

A special thanks to those who allowed me to tell their stories. You have helped me to illustrate truth and inspire courage. Thanks to Lee and Rhonda Sleiter, Scott and Jeannie Thomas, and others whose names and some details were changed for the sake of preference or prudence. And, of course, Dr. David Powlison, thank you for the amazing nested circles diagram in chapter 2. Your life and ministry reflect the gospel scope those circles portray.

I think I better understand grace these days. In other words, I better understand how little I know. But for what I do see and for any light this book offers in opening eyes or helping marriages, I thank Jesus. In all I have done or will do, he alone is the only thing worth seeing or remembering.

**Dave Harvey** (DMin, Westminster Theological Seminary) serves as the president of Great Commission Collective, a church planting ministry in the US, Canada, and abroad. Dave founded Am ICalled.com, pastored for thirty-three years, serves on the board of CCEF, and travels widely across networks and denominations as a popular conference speaker. He is the author of *When Sinners Say "I Do"*; *Am I Called?*; and *Rescuing Ambition*, and a coauthor of *Letting Go: Rugged Love for Wayward Souls*. He and his wife, Kimm, have four kids and four grandchildren and live in southwest Florida. For videos, articles, or to book an event, visit www.revdaveharvey.com.

# Connect with
# DAVE!

To discover more content from Dave Harvey and find more resources for marriage and ministry, visit

## RevDaveHarvey.com

  @RevDaveHarvey

Connect with
**BakerBooks**
Relevant. Intelligent. Engaging.

Sign up for announcements about
new and upcoming titles at

**BakerBooks.com/SignUp**

@ReadBakerBooks